ADVANCING SCIENTIFIC RESEARCH IN EDUCATION

D1521581

Committee on Research in Education

Lisa Towne, Lauress L. Wise, and Tina M. Winters, Editors

Center for Education

Division of Behavioral and Social Sciences and Education

NATIONAL RESEARCH COUNCIL
OF THE NATIONAL ACADEMIES

THE NATIONAL ACADEMIES PRESS
Washington, D.C.
www.nap.edu

THE NATIONAL ACADEMIES PRESS 500 Fifth Street, N.W. Washington, DC 20001

NOTICE: The project that is the subject of this report was approved by the Governing Board of the National Research Council, whose members are drawn from the councils of the National Academy of Sciences, the National Academy of Engineering, and the Institute of Medicine. The members of the committee responsible for the report were chosen for their special competences and with regard for appropriate balance.

This study was supported by Contract No. ED-00-CO-0088 between the National Academy of Sciences and the U.S. Department of Education, Grant No. 2002-7860 from the William and Flora Hewlett Foundation, and Grant No. 200200225 from the Spencer Foundation. Any opinions, findings, conclusions, or recommendations expressed in this publication are those of the authors and do not necessarily reflect the views of the U.S. Department of Education, the William and Flora Hewlett Foundation, or the Spencer Foundation.

Library of Congress Cataloging-in-Publication Data

National Research Council (U.S.). Committee on Research in Education.
  Advancing scientific research in education / Committee on Research in Education ; Lisa Towne, Lauress L. Wise, and Tina M. Winters, editors.
    p. cm.
  Includes bibliographical references.
  ISBN 0-309-09321-X (pbk.) — ISBN 0-309-54598-6 (pdf)
  1. Education—Research—United States. I. Towne, Lisa. II. Wise, Lauress L. III. Winters, Tina M. IV. Title.
  LB1028.25.U6N373 2004
  370'.7'2—dc22
                              2004026249

Additional copies of this report are available from National Academies Press, 500 Fifth Street, N.W., Lockbox 285, Washington, DC 20055; (800) 624-6242 or (202) 334-3313 (in the Washington metropolitan area); Internet, http://www.nap.edu.

Suggested citation: National Research Council. (2005). *Advancing Scientific Research in Education.* Committee on Research in Education. Lisa Towne, Lauress L. Wise, and Tina M. Winters, Editors. Center for Education, Division of Behavioral and Social Sciences and Education. Washington, DC: The National Academies Press.

THE NATIONAL ACADEMIES
Advisers to the Nation on Science, Engineering, and Medicine

The **National Academy of Sciences** is a private, nonprofit, self-perpetuating society of distinguished scholars engaged in scientific and engineering research, dedicated to the furtherance of science and technology and to their use for the general welfare. Upon the authority of the charter granted to it by the Congress in 1863, the Academy has a mandate that requires it to advise the federal government on scientific and technical matters. Dr. Bruce M. Alberts is president of the National Academy of Sciences.

The **National Academy of Engineering** was established in 1964, under the charter of the National Academy of Sciences, as a parallel organization of outstanding engineers. It is autonomous in its administration and in the selection of its members, sharing with the National Academy of Sciences the responsibility for advising the federal government. The National Academy of Engineering also sponsors engineering programs aimed at meeting national needs, encourages education and research, and recognizes the superior achievements of engineers. Dr. Wm. A. Wulf is president of the National Academy of Engineering.

The **Institute of Medicine** was established in 1970 by the National Academy of Sciences to secure the services of eminent members of appropriate professions in the examination of policy matters pertaining to the health of the public. The Institute acts under the responsibility given to the National Academy of Sciences by its congressional charter to be an adviser to the federal government and, upon its own initiative, to identify issues of medical care, research, and education. Dr. Harvey V. Fineberg is president of the Institute of Medicine.

The **National Research Council** was organized by the National Academy of Sciences in 1916 to associate the broad community of science and technology with the Academy's purposes of furthering knowledge and advising the federal government. Functioning in accordance with general policies determined by the Academy, the Council has become the principal operating agency of both the National Academy of Sciences and the National Academy of Engineering in providing services to the government, the public, and the scientific and engineering communities. The Council is administered jointly by both Academies and the Institute of Medicine. Dr. Bruce M. Alberts and Dr. Wm. A. Wulf are chair and vice chair, respectively, of the National Research Council.

www.national-academies.org

v

Preface

The central idea of evidence-based education—that education policy and practice ought to be fashioned based on what is known from rigorous research—offers a compelling way to approach reform efforts. Recent federal trends reflect a growing enthusiasm for such change. Most visibly, the No Child Left Behind Act requires that "scientifically based [education] research" drive the use of federal education funds at the state and local levels. This emphasis is also reflected in a number of government and nongovernment initiatives across the country. As consensus builds around the goals of evidence-based education, consideration of what it will take to make it a reality becomes the crucial next step.

In this context, the Center for Education of the National Research Council (NRC) has undertaken a series of activities to address issues related to the quality of scientific education research.[1] In 2002, the NRC released *Scientific Research in Education* (National Research Council, 2002), a report designed to articulate the nature of scientific education research and to guide efforts aimed at improving its quality. Building on this work, the Committee on Research in Education was convened to advance an improved understanding of a scientific approach to addressing education prob-

---

[1]Other NRC efforts—especially the line of work that culminated in the recent report *Strategic Education Research Partnership* (National Research Council, 2003b)—offer insights and advice about ways to advance research utilization more broadly.

lems; to engage the field of education research in action-oriented dialogue about how to further the accumulation of scientific knowledge; and to coordinate, support, and promote cross-fertilization among NRC efforts in education research.

The main locus of activity undertaken to meet these objectives was a year-long series of workshops to engage a range of education stakeholders in discussions about five key topics. Since these events provide the basis for the committee's conclusions and recommendations, we wish to acknowledge and thank speakers[2] from each of the events for their extremely helpful contributions to our deliberations:

• *Peer Review in Federal Education Research Programs.* This workshop focused on the purposes and practices of peer review in many of the federal agencies that fund education research. Federal officials and researchers considered a range of models used across the government to involve peers in the review of proposals for education research funding and discussed ways to foster a high-quality portfolio. It took place on February 25-26, 2003, at the Keck Center of the National Academies in Washington, DC. A report of this event was issued in July 2004 and contains the committee's conclusions and recommendations about peer review in federal agencies that support education research. It can be viewed at http://books.nap.edu/catalog/11054.html.

Speakers included Diane August, August and Associates; Hilda Borko, University of Colorado, Boulder; Steven Breckler, National Science Foundation; Susan Chipman, Office of Naval Research; Dominic Cicchetti, Yale University; Louis Danielson, Office of Special Education Programs, U.S. Department of Education; Kenneth Dodge, Duke University; Edward Hackett, Arizona State University; Milton Hakel, Bowling Green State University; Teresa Levitin, National Institutes of Health; Penelope Peterson, Northwestern University; Edward Reddish, University of Maryland; Finbarr Sloane, National Science Foundation; Brent Stanfield, National Institutes of Health; Robert Sternberg, Yale University; and Grover (Russ) Whitehurst, Institute of Education Sciences.

• *Understanding and Promoting Knowledge Accumulation in Education: Tools and Strategies for Education Research.* With a focus on how to build a

---

[2]For each speaker, we provide their affiliation at the time of the workshop.

coherent knowledge base in education research, researchers and federal officials considered several elements of the research infrastructure, including tools, practices, models, and standards. Fundamental questions about what such a knowledge base might look like were also considered in this context. It took place on June 30-July 1, 2003, at the main building of the National Academies in Washington, DC. A summary of this event appears in this report as Appendix B.

Speakers included Daniel Berch, National Institutes of Health; Norman Bradburn, National Science Foundation; Claudia Buchmann, Duke University; David K. Cohen, University of Michigan; Harris Cooper, Duke University; Ronald Ehrenberg, Cornell University; David Grissmer, RAND Corporation; Kenji Hakuta, University of California, Merced; Kenneth Howe, University of Colorado, Boulder; Jay Labov, National Research Council; Helen (Sunny) Ladd, Duke University; David McQueen, Centers for Disease Control and Prevention; Hugh (Bud) Mehan, University of California, San Diego; Gary Natriello, Columbia University; Michael Nettles, Educational Testing Service; Barbara Rogoff, University of California, Santa Cruz; Barbara Schneider, University of Chicago; Marilyn McMillen Seastrom, National Center for Education Statistics; Robert Slavin, Johns Hopkins University and the Success for All Foundation; Sidney Winter, University of Pennsylvania; and Lauress L. Wise, HumRRO.

• *Random Assignment Experimentation in Education: Implementation and Implications.* The evidence-based education trend has brought to the fore decades of debate about the appropriateness of randomized field trials in education. Far less consideration has been devoted to the practical aspects of conducting such studies in educational settings; this workshop featured detailed descriptions of the implementation of studies using randomized field trials in education and reflections on how the current trend to fund more of these studies is influencing states, districts, and students. It took place on September 24, 2003, at the Keck Center of the National Academies in Washington, DC. A summary of this event was issued in May 2004 and can be viewed at http://books.nap.edu/catalog/10943.html.

Speakers included Robert F. Boruch, University of Pennsylvania; Wesley Bruce, Indiana Department of Education; Linda Chinnia, Baltimore City Public School System; Donna Durno, Allegheny Intermediate Unit; Olatokunbo S. Fashola, Johns Hopkins University; Judith Gueron, MDRC; Vinetta C. Jones, Howard University; Sheppard Kellam, American Institutes for Research; Anthony (Eamonn) Kelly, George Mason University; Sharon Lewis, Council of the Great City Schools; Loretta McClairn, Baltimore City Public School System; David Myers, Mathematica Policy Research; and Richard J. Shavelson, Stanford University.

• *Journal Practices in Publishing Education Research.* Following the more general discussion of how to build a coherent knowledge base in education in a previous workshop, this event took up the specific case of journals that publish education research. Editors, publication committee members, and others involved in the production and use of journal articles considered ways to promote high-quality education research and to contribute to the larger body of knowledge about important areas of policy and practice. It took place on November 11, 2003, at the Wyndham City Center in Washington, DC.

Speakers included Bridget Coughlin, National Academy of Sciences; Catherine Emihovich, University of Florida; Glenn Firebaugh, Pennsylvania State University; Lynn Liben, Pennsylvania State University; Margaret McKeown, University of Pittsburgh; Gary Natriello, Columbia University; Hannah Rothstein, City University of New York; Barbara Schneider, University of Chicago; Judith Sebba, University of Sussex; Gary VandenBos, American Psychological Association; and John Willinsky, University of British Columbia.

• *Education Doctoral Programs for Future Leaders in Education Research.* A final workshop focused on the professional development of education researchers, with a specific emphasis on doctoral programs in schools of education. Deans, graduate study coordinators, foundation officials, and policy makers came together to share observations and chart potential paths for progress. It took place on November 12, 2003, at the Wyndham City Center in Washington, DC.

Speakers included David K. Cohen, University of Michigan; Margaret Eisenhart, University of Colorado, Boulder; Charles Hancock, Ohio State University; David Labaree, Stanford University; Felice Levine, American Educational Research Association; Steven Raudenbush, University of Michigan; Lee Shulman, Carnegie Foundation for the Advancement of Teaching; Joseph Tobin, Arizona State University; and Grover (Russ) Whitehurst, Institute of Education Sciences.

Additional information on each of these events and speakers, including transcripts of each workshop, can be found at http://www7. nationalacademies.org/core/. Appendix A is a compilation of the workshop agendas. This report is a synthesis of themes and recommendations that emerged from the workshop series viewed as a whole.

Of course, without the generous support of our sponsors, neither the workshop series nor this report would be possible. We extend our gratitude to the former National Educational Research Policy and Priorities Board and the Institute of Education Sciences, the William and Flora Hewlett Foundation, and the Spencer Foundation for their support and guidance.

We extend our thanks to each of the members of the Committee on Research in Education (see Appendix C for biographical sketches). We especially appreciate the efforts of the workshop planning groups, who designed a series of outstanding events on important topics in education research and policy. Several NRC staff played critical roles in shaping the workshops and deserve special recognition: Tina M. Winters served as the research associate throughout the project, applying her considerable talents to a range of project tasks, including the development of the knowledge accumulation workshop; Meryl Bertenthal ably led the staff effort in developing the agenda for the peer review workshop. And we thank Christine McShane and Eugenia Grohman for their skillful editing of the manuscript.

This report has been reviewed in draft form by individuals chosen for their diverse perspectives and technical expertise, in accordance with procedures approved by the NRC's Report Review Committee. The purpose of this independent review is to provide candid and critical comments that will assist the institution in making its published report as sound as possible and to ensure that the report meets institutional standards for objectivity, evidence, and responsiveness to the study charge. The review comments and draft manuscript remain confidential to protect the integrity of the deliberative process.

We wish to thank the following individuals for their review of this report: Mary E. Dilworth, Research and Information Services, American Association of Colleges for Teacher Education, Washington, DC; Emerson J. Elliott, Program Standards Development Project, National Council for the Accreditation of Teacher Education, Washington, DC; Gary J. Natriello, Department of Sociology and Education, Teachers College, Columbia University; Penelope L. Peterson, School of Education and Social Policy, Northwestern University; Barbara Rogoff, Department of Psychology, University of California, Santa Cruz; Nora Sabelli, Center for Technology and Learning, SRI International, Menlo Park, CA; Morton M. Sternheim, STEM Education Institute, University of Massachusetts,

Amherst; Jeanine P. Wiener-Kronish, Department of Anesthesia and Perioperative Care, Cardiovascular Research Institute, University of California, San Francisco; Suzanne M. Wilson, Department of Teacher Education, Center for the Scholarship of Teaching, Michigan State University; Mary Yakimowski, Research, Evaluation and Accountability Department, Baltimore City Public Schools.

Although the reviewers listed above have provided many constructive comments and suggestions, they were not asked to endorse the conclusions or recommendations, nor did they see the final draft of the report before its release. The review of this report was overseen by Robert L. Linn, School of Education, University of Colorado, Boulder. Appointed by the National Research Council, he was responsible for making certain that an independent examination of this report was carried out in accordance with institutional procedures and that all review comments were carefully considered. Responsibility for the final content of this report rests entirely with the authoring committee and the institution.

Lauress L. Wise, *Chair*
Lisa Towne, *Study Director*
Committee on Research in Education

Contents

EXECUTIVE SUMMARY   1

1   INTRODUCTION   9
Context and Rationale, 9
Strands of Work, 11
Sources of Evidence and Nature of Recommendations, 14
Defining the Parameters, 15
Target Audience, 16
Strategic Objectives, 17

2   PROMOTING QUALITY   19
Elements of Quality, 20
Mechanisms for Promoting Quality, 22
Conclusion, 33

3   BUILDING THE KNOWLEDGE BASE   36
Framing Concepts, 36
Mechanisms for Building the Knowledge Base, 38
Conclusion, 55

4   ENHANCING PROFESSIONAL DEVELOPMENT   56
Nature of the Field, 56
Mechanisms for Enhancing Professional Development, 57
Conclusion, 71

5   SUMMARY AND CONCLUSION   72
    Recommendations, 72
    Recommendations by Target Audience, 74
    Issues for Future Consideration, 77
    Conclusion, 80

REFERENCES   81

APPENDIXES
A   Workshop Agendas   87
B   Understanding and Promoting Knowledge Accumulation:
    Summary of Workshop Key Points   97
C   Biographical Sketches of Committee Members and Staff   115

ADVANCING
SCIENTIFIC RESEARCH
IN EDUCATION

Executive Summary

The title of this report reveals its purpose precisely: to spur actions that will advance scientific research in education. Our recommendations for accomplishing this goal build on the National Research Council report *Scientific Research in Education*. That report offered an articulation of what constitutes high-quality scientific inquiry in education; this report recommends ways to promote it.

Two pieces of recent federal legislation—the No Child Left Behind Act of 2001 and the Education Sciences Reform Act of 2002—have catapulted education research into the spotlight. Both acts are premised on the idea that education research can and should contribute to policy and practice, that education should be an evidence-based field. At the same time, the inclusion of definitions of what constitutes "scientifically based research" in both acts reflects deep skepticism about the quality and rigor of education research.

Some education research lacks quality, just as does some research in medicine, neuroscience, economics, or any other field. It is not necessary to denigrate or to defend the field on this point. The point is that scientific research in education can be improved, and the field should focus its energies on doing so.

The National Research Council convened the Committee on Research in Education to foster high-level dialogue with key participants in education research to promote such improvements. To carry out this task, the committee organized a five-part workshop series and published several reports on selected topics.

In this final report, we offer recommendations for improving scientific research in education, organized around three strategic objectives: promoting quality, building the knowledge base, and enhancing the professional development of researchers. This is a time of unprecedented opportunity for education researchers to initiate bold reforms. The enthusiasm—and angst—surrounding recent calls for "scientifically based research" can and should be harnessed to advance the field of education research. The time to act is now.

PROMOTING QUALITY

The intellectual predecessor to this report, *Scientific Research in Education,* was an attempt to articulate what is meant by quality with respect to scientific research in education. The definition is a combination of six guiding principles that underlie all scientific fields, along with several features of education that shape how these principles apply to research on teaching, learning, and schooling. We adopted that framework as our working definition of quality of scientific education research.

Recently, much attention has been focused on "upgrading" the methods used in education studies, with a particular emphasis on randomized field trials to help establish cause-and-effect relationships. Methodologies are the tools researchers use to do their work; their appropriate use is essential to promoting quality. However, matching appropriate methods to research questions is a necessary but not sufficient condition for ensuring scientific rigor. We conclude that the national conversation about methodological quality is but a part of a needed broader focus on how to define and uphold quality in scientific education research. Issues such as the development of theory and the use of replications to clarify generalizability are examples of aspects of scientific quality that are equally important to consider.

Our recommendations for ways to promote quality—broadly defined— focus on peer review systems in federal agencies that support education research, the implementation of research designs in school settings, and partnerships between researchers and school personnel.

Recommendation 1. In federal agencies that support education research, the criteria by which peer reviewers rate proposals should be clearly delineated, and the meaning of different score levels on each scale should be defined and illustrated. Reviewers should be trained in the use of these scales. Defining, revisiting, and upholding standards of quality in the peer review process enhances the development of high-quality education research over time by facilitating reliable and valid ratings of proposals for funding and feedback to applicants.

Recommendation 2. Federal agencies that support education research should ensure that as a group, each peer review panel has the research experience and expertise to judge the theoretical and technical merits of the proposals it reviews. In addition, peer review panels should be composed so as to minimize conflicts of interest, to balance biases, and to promote the participation of people from a range of scholarly perspectives and traditionally underrepresented groups. The group of peer reviewers assembled to judge education research proposals should have the expertise to judge the content areas of the proposed work, the methods and analytic techniques proposed to address the research question, and the policy and practice contexts in which the work is situated. Agency staff should seek to eliminate conflicts of interest among reviewers. However, because many of the best reviewers are likely to have some association with applicants, overly restrictive conflict of interest rules can dramatically shrink the pool of competent reviewers. Biases among peer reviewers need not be eliminated, but rather must be identified, discussed among the group, and balanced across panelists. Ensuring a breadth of perspectives in peer review panels promotes high-quality reviews over time by engaging different kinds of expertise and insights around a common set of proposals, issues, and evaluation criteria.

Recommendation 3. In research conducted in educational settings, investigators must not only select rigorous methods appropriate to the questions posed but also implement them in ways that meet the highest standards of evidence for those questions and methods. The choice of research design and method must be driven by the particulars of the question posed for investigation. The implementation of the design in school settings is equally important: challenges arise in working with schools, and strategies must be in place to anticipate them and to solve unanticipated problems as they arise. Partnerships between the research team and school personnel facilitate effective implementation.

Recommendation 4. Federal agencies should ensure appropriate resources are available for education researchers conducting large-scale investigations in educational settings to build partnerships with practitioners and policy makers. Time and money are needed to develop the partnerships necessary to ensure effective implementation of large-scale education research studies. Research project budgets should provide such resources.

BUILDING THE KNOWLEDGE BASE

Even if the quality of discrete education research projects has been ensured, if the field lacks the will or the tools to forge connections among studies, it will amass a multitude of studies that cannot support inferences about generalizability nor sustain the theory building that underlies scientific progress. We conclude that greater attention must be paid to reanalysis, replication, and testing the boundaries of theories with empirical inquiries, as well as to taking stock of what is known in areas of interest to education policy and practice on a regular basis.

Our recommendations for building the knowledge base focus on data sharing, infrastructure development, and journal policies.

Recommendation 5. Professional associations involved in education research should develop explicit ethical standards for data sharing. The American Educational Research Association and similar groups should be at the forefront of efforts to promote the sharing of education-related data among qualified investigators to enable reanalyses, replications, and further investigation with available data. Ethical standards should consider how to ensure the confidentiality of research participants, especially with qualitative data. The rights and protections of authors should also be specified.

Recommendation 6. Education research journals should require authors to make relevant data available to other researchers as a condition of publication and to ensure that applicable ethical standards are upheld. Cultural barriers and institutional disincentives that work against data sharing and related practices should be addressed candidly and reformed thoughtfully.

Recommendation 7. Professional associations and education research journals should work in concert with funding agencies to create an infrastructure that takes advantage of technology to facilitate data sharing and knowledge accumulation in education research. Promising mechanisms include data repositories, registries of initiated studies, bibliographic indexes of published studies, digitization of journal content, and open access.

Recommendation 8. Education research journals should develop and implement policies to require structured abstracts. Abstracts are used in the development of systematic reviews of multiple education studies on similar topics to identify the universe of relevant research. To facilitate these reviews and to promote better access to relevant studies among the many consumers of education research, all abstracts should contain basic information about the purpose, sample strategy, methodology, and other key features of the investigation.

ENHANCING PROFESSIONAL DEVELOPMENT

A diverse pool of well-trained education researchers is needed to contribute to deliberations about educational practice and policy in response to the complex questions being asked of education research. The question is: Are existing training and professional development activities sufficient to produce a capable cadre of investigators and to respond to the demands of practitioners and policy makers?

Our recommendations for improving the professional development of education researchers focus on doctoral programs in schools of education, and the peer review systems in both federal agencies and in journals.

Recommendation 9. Schools of education that train doctoral students for careers in education research should articulate the competencies those graduates should know and be able to do and design their programs to enable students to develop them. The articulation of competencies is essential for designing course work, organizing research experiences, and developing other program elements. Such an exercise would also define a minimum breadth of skills all would-be education researchers should have. This articulation may require differentiation within programs of schools of education, such as educational psychology and curriculum and instruction.

Recommendation 10. Schools of education that train doctoral students for careers in education research should design their programs to enable those students to develop deep substantive and methodological knowledge and skill in a specialized area. As students progress through their doctoral training, their course work and research experiences should hone their skills and understanding in the theoretical ideas, methodological tools, and existing research in the particular area in education research they intend to pursue. Interdepartmental collaborations can often facilitate in-depth training by providing opportunities for students to explore areas and to work with faculty outside schools of education.

Recommendation 11. Schools of education that train doctoral students for careers in education research should provide those students with a variety of meaningful research experiences. Research experience while in training is absolutely essential to a research career. Staging a series of research experiences over the course of doctoral study facilitates the development of research skills and provides opportunities for publishing research findings in peer-reviewed journals, presenting at conferences, and participating in other activities that are the foundation of the profession. Ensuring meaningful research experiences for doctoral students requires that they engage in research under the guidance of multiple faculty members who themselves are active in the field.

Recommendation 12. Peer review panels in federal agencies that fund education research should be composed to promote the participation of people from a range of scholarly perspectives and traditionally underrepresented groups and provide opportunities for professional development. Although not typically viewed as a vehicle for professional growth, properly designed peer review experiences can provide opportunities for interaction, feedback, and interdisciplinary conversations that promote learning among applicants, reviewers, and agency staff. Such design features as standing panels, which enable interactions over time, and clear and consistent feedback to applicants can be effective ways to promote this professional development.

Recommendation 13. Publishers of peer-reviewed education research should design their editorial and manuscript review systems to promote the professional development of education researchers who participate in that process. Just as peer review of research proposals can be an enriching experience for those involved, so too can the process of judging manuscripts submitted to journals for publication. Opportunities for editors, authors, and reviewers to benefit from each others' ideas and critiques should be maximized.

We call on the three major institutions to which these recommendations are addressed—federal funding agencies, schools of education and universities, and professional associations—to work together towards promoting quality, building the knowledge base, and enhancing the professional development of researchers. A shared commitment among them can lead to the partnerships, strategic investments, and infrastructure support needed to advance scientific research in education.

1

Introduction

The title of this report reveals its purpose precisely: to spur actions that will advance scientific research in education. The recommendations for accomplishing this goal, detailed in the pages that follow, build on the National Research Council (NRC) report *Scientific Research in Education* (National Research Council, 2002). That report offered an articulation of what constitutes high-quality scientific inquiry into education; this report recommends ways to promote it.

CONTEXT AND RATIONALE

The field of education research as a distinct area of scholarly inquiry has evolved over roughly 100 years. It comprises a group of investigators from different disciplines, fields, and institutions who bring a range of theories, objectives, and orientations to their work. It is grounded in the social and behavioral sciences, but it lacks a disciplinary framework like those that shape the academic study of anthropology, or economics, or psychology. More akin in some ways to professional fields like social work or public policy, education research takes cues from the practice of teaching, the process of learning, and the organizational structures and routines of the many institutions with education-related missions. Sharing commonalities among these related scientific and professional fields, education research nonetheless bears its own distinctions as a field of study. Indeed, since its earliest days, education researchers have debated the core nature of education research given the complexity of the subject and the diversity of the field of investigators.

Recent changes in the education policy landscape have drawn these debates out of the exclusive realm of academe, making for especially interesting times for education research. The proliferation of standards-based reforms and high-stakes accountability regimes over the past 20 years has slowly but steadily built demand for research "proven" strategies among educators.[1] Most recently, two pieces of federal legislation—the No Child Left Behind Act of 2001 and the Education Sciences Reform Act of 2002—have catapulted education research into the spotlight, with as yet unknown effects.

Both acts are premised on the idea that education research can and should shape policy and practice or, as the Department of Education's Strategic Plan puts it, education should be "transformed into an evidence-based field" (U.S. Department of Education, 2002b). Key decision makers involved in crafting these policies often frame the issue this way: if patients expect that their physician's practice is informed by the best available research evidence, why shouldn't parents expect that teachers and administrators are delivering instruction and organizing learning environments in the same way? Evidence-based medicine is not as widespread a trend as one might expect or hope (Sackett, Richardson, Rosenberg, and Haynes, 1997; Institute of Medicine, 2001), and education is like and unlike medicine in complex ways. But evidence-based education is a comparatively new trend (National Research Council, 1999).

The explicit coupling of research and reform in federal education law has spurred a range of reactions and actions among education researchers. Some have attempted to seize the opportunity and work to promote the goals of evidence-based education. Others are troubled by the problems they see with these policies, focusing on the fact that both education laws

---

[1]Legislative requirements to rely on research for programmatic decisions first appeared in the Reading Excellence Act and the Comprehensive School Reform Demonstration Act in the mid- to late-1990s. Former U.S. Representative Bill Goodling (R-PA) introduced a bill in 1997 with references to "scientifically based research"; the Reading Excellence Act became law a year later. Guided by the leadership of U.S. Representative David Obey (D-WI) and former U.S. Representative John Porter (R-IL), the Comprehensive School Reform Demonstration (CSRD) program that was created in the 1997 appropriations process under the federal Title I program, also included language about "reliable, replicable research" (Towne, in press).

define legislatively (politically) what constitutes "scientifically based research" and expressing concern about what they view as an inappropriate encroachment on their profession.

In late 2000, when the reauthorization of the U.S. Office of Educational Research and Improvement was first under consideration by Congress (these and subsequent deliberations would eventually lead to the passage of the Education Sciences Reform Act of 2002), the NRC was approached to bring the expertise of education researchers and other scientists to bear on the complex question of how to characterize scientifically based research in education. The result was the publication *Scientific Research in Education* (National Research Council, 2002), which was authored by a group of researchers and intended to provide a scholarly rendering of the major issues and terms that had made their way into the standard rhetoric of education policy makers. There is some evidence to suggest that the book influenced revisions that were made to the definition of scientifically based research in the Education Sciences Reform Act (Eisenhart and Towne, 2003).

Regardless of the content of such definitions of scientifically based research that appear in education law, the inclusion of such definitions in federal statutes reflects a deep skepticism about the quality and rigor of education scholarship. So, too, have some scholars expressed deep concern about a lack of quality in education research (Kaestle, 1993; Levin and O'Donnell, 1999; Carnine, 2000; Vaughn and Damann, 2001). It is almost certain that some education research lacks quality, just as it is almost certain that some medical research, some biological research, and some neuroscience research lack quality. It is not necessary to denigrate or to defend the field on this point. What matters is that the current landscape offers a ripe opportunity for self-reflection and improvement, and that is our point of departure: *scientific research in education could be improved, and the field should focus its energies on doing so.*

STRANDS OF WORK

The NRC convened the Committee on Research in Education to foster high-level dialogue with key participants in education research to promote such improvements. The committee embarked on two related strands of work to accomplish this objective: a five-part workshop series to engage a wide range of scholars, policy makers, and educators in an action-oriented dialogue to clarify issues and to discuss ways in which current practice could be improved, and a series of reports on selected topics raised in the workshop series.

As described in more detail in the preface, the topic areas for the workshop series include peer review in federal agencies that support education research, strategies to promote the development of a knowledge base in education, implementation of randomized field trials in educational settings, the role of journals in contributing to a knowledge base in education, and doctoral programs for education researchers. The committee's web site (http://www7.nationalacademies.org/core/) features a page dedicated to each of the events held on these topics. For a given event, an agenda with hyperlinks, broken down by presentation, enables easy viewing of biographical information about the speakers, Powerpoint slides if used, and (in most cases) verbatim transcripts of speaker remarks and audience participation.

The committee selected the workshop topics on the basis of a number of related factors. First, they were issues our sponsors were interested in pursuing as points of leverage for improvements in scientific education research. For example, recognizing that the federal government was poised to fund many more randomized field trials in education than had been conducted at any other time in history, the former National Educational Research Policy and Priorities Board was interested in implementation issues associated with such studies; therefore, the committee brought researchers and practitioners together to share best practices about how these types of studies can be successfully implemented in real-world educational settings. The William and Flora Hewlett Foundation invested in the committee's work as well, charging us with focusing on concrete ways to facilitate a more integrated knowledge base in education, including the role that journals might play; thus, we convened workshops to discuss several potential strategies for promoting knowledge accumulation, including journal policies and practices.

A second factor we considered in designing the individual workshops was how the themes and ideas contained in *Scientific Research in Education* could be extended. For example, that book stressed the importance of a culture of scientific rigor among the field of investigators in promoting high-quality education research, and we designed the final workshop to focus on one key lever for instilling that culture and developing capacity: doctoral training in schools of education of future leaders in education research.

We also considered what topics were of particular salience to education policy issues. Peer review, for example, is a concept that is featured in the definitions of "scientifically based research" in both the No Child Left Behind Act and the Education Sciences Reform Act and of course, a longstanding practice in many scholarly fields to promote high-quality reseach. Two of our workshops therefore focused on the role of peer review: one focused on peer review as it is used in federal agencies to vet proposals for research funding, and one included discussion of the review of manuscripts submitted to journals for publication. Overall, the series touched on a wide range of important issues and ideas and provided rich fodder for discussion and for the development of this report. We cannot claim, however, that we have conducted an exhaustive analysis, nor that these recommendations are the only ways scientific research in education could be improved.

With the publication of this report, we have issued three reports based on select topics in the workshop series. The first two, *Implementing Randomized Field Trials in Education: Report of a Workshop* (National Research Council, 2004a; available: http://books.nap.edu/catalog/10943.html) and *Strengthening Peer Review in Federal Agencies That Support Education Research* (National Research Council, 2004b; available: http://books.nap.edu/catalog/11042.html) are based on specific workshop discussions and issues. We chose to issue these two topical reports based on our judgment of the issues as most pressing and promising in the education policy and research circles. Randomized field trials have dominated much of the policy debate in the past few years, but since little had been written about implementation issues, we chose to issue a short report that summarized our workshop on the topic. Further, the Education Sciences Reform Act called for the formation of a new policy board—the National Board of Education Sciences—which will work with the director of the Institute of Education Sciences (IES) to formulate and oversee the agency's peer review system. Thus, we issued a report that contains conclusions and recommendations about peer review systems in federal agencies that support education research (including, but not limited to IES) to be useful to such officials charged with developing or revamping peer review systems in the near future.

Over the course of the workshop series, common themes emerged from the discussions of a fairly diverse set of topics. This final report reflects those cross-cutting themes and ideas and points to a set of strategies the committee views as most promising for promoting targeted improvements in scientific research in education. It is therefore organized around major themes from across the workshops, rather than by workshop topic.

SOURCES OF EVIDENCE AND
NATURE OF RECOMMENDATIONS

The primary source of evidence for the conclusions and recommendations in this report is the presentations and discussions that took place in the workshop series. The committee designed these events to promote broad-based discussions of a range of complex issues in education among leading scholars in the field. Each event included ample time for the committee to ask questions of presenters, as well as for audience members to ask questions and to add their perspectives.

We also draw on our own collective experience as researchers and practitioners in education and other fields. Together, we have held several leadership positions in many of the key organizations we target, including journals, professional associations, and schools of education. These experiences supplement the workshop dialogue to support the conclusions and recommendations.

Drawing primarily on workshop discussions to support our conclusions and recommendations has important implications for the nature of the committee's recommendations and for how we treat and use this type of evidence in the report. Because the kinds of issues raised in the workshop series and the associated underlying knowledge bases about them vary, so, too, do our recommendations. In most cases, the recommendations are statements of critical objectives to be pursued by the field with suggestions for possible mechanisms; in others, they contain specific strategies for action by specific organizations. This variability reflects the fact that the workshops themselves were designed to be explorations of major issues related to education research to build on—but not complete—the work of the committee that authored *Scientific Research in Education.* We also selectively chose ideas and strategies raised during the workshop series that we judge as most important to highlight and to pursue. Thus, the committee offers targeted recommendations to be considered broadly and implemented intelligently over time. Our goal is to push the conversation to the next level and to spur positive change.

Throughout the report, we offer examples from our workshops of issues related to and practices of federal agencies, professional associations, schools of education, and journals (our target audiences; see page 16).

These practices, however, are not necessarily representative, and do not constitute the thorough baseline assessment that will be needed to implement change effectively over time. That work remains to be done.

A similar caveat relates to the costs associated with implementing the recommendations. Cost estimates were rarely available, and indeed, because many of the committee's recommendations are framed broadly, estimating cost would entail the development of more detailed plans for action. There is no doubt that new resources will be needed and that implementation will need to take place incrementally as resources become available. Implementing the recommendations effectively will take strategic investments that leverage existing resources and build capacity in and across organizations over time.

Since the committee's primary source of evidence for our recommendations is this series of events and discussions, throughout the report we formally cite specific workshop speakers. Corresponding to these citations in the text, the reference list contains information about the date and topic area of each workshop and a link to the transcript of the specific presentation referenced from the committee's website. This website also contains short biographical sketches of each presenter, as well as more detailed information about the committee and its work.

DEFINING THE PARAMETERS

The focus in the workshop series, and therefore in this report, is on scientific research in education. As a committee of the NRC—the operating arm of the National Academy of Sciences—a basic premise of our work is that the pursuit of scientific understanding can be a powerful tool for the betterment of society. The committee approached the task of recommending strategies for improving scientific research in education with the strong belief that it can and should be used to improve education policy and practice.

Steadfast in this belief, we also recognize and respect that scholarly inquiry in the social sciences and education is not limited to scientific approaches. Indeed, *Scientific Research in Education* (National Research Council, 2002)—a book we did not author but that has shaped our work— proved to be controversial among some education researchers, for three main reasons. Critics faulted the book for accepting uncritically the premise that scientific research in education is possible and worthwhile, for depicting a flawed or outmoded view of what constituted scientific inquiry into education phenomena, or for being silent on the role of politics in defining scientifically based research in education (Erickson and Guitterez, 2002; St. Pierre, 2002; Eisenhart and Towne, 2003).

Given these controversies, we think it is our responsibility to convey that there is more than one way to view the world and that science is not universally applicable to understanding all issues relevant to education or its improvement. Since the committee's charge was to address ways in which *scientific* education research could be improved, however, we do not consider the relative merits or contributions of approaches to education research that do not define themselves as scientific, approaches that include such disparate paradigms as interpretivism, postmodernism, and critical theory.

The committee's own epistemological and theoretical orientations—which vary among the members—clearly shape how we went about our work. We do not attempt to systematically explore these issues or to adopt a single framework, however. Rather, we have taken the insights and ideas generated at the workshops and worked together to reach consensus on a set of strategies that collectively we think can advance scientific education research, as well as for its use in promoting improvements in education policy and practice.

In addition, the focus of the report is on improving the capacity of the research communities to provide a scientific basis for proposed reforms and other policy decisions that affect education. We do not take up the complex question of how to promote the utilization of education research in ways that improve educational outcomes. That said, the two are inextricably linked. Indeed, there are places throughout the report where we consider the nexus between quality and utility quite explicitly. Thus, while the overarching goal is to facilitate research-based reform, we primarily tackle the "supply" side of the equation—that is, how to strengthen the quality of scientific education research, without directly addressing the "demand" side—that is, how to promote effective use of that research as a crucial part of the formulation and implementation of policy and practice.

TARGET AUDIENCE

The primary audience for this report is education researchers and the institutions that support them—universities, federal agencies, professional associations, and foundations. Since the focus is on advancing scientific research in education, these are the people and organizations most central to the effective implementation of the recommendations the committee proposes. We found over the course of our deliberations—and know from our own work and experience—that it is often unclear where to target reform efforts in the field of education research. A multitude of participants and decision makers overlap in their authority, responsibility, and power, and existing incentives often work against change. We have attempted to focus the recommendations on major institutional leverage points, and in the final chapter, we provide a summary of these recommendations categorized by audience.

We also think that education policy makers involved in implementing evidence-based reforms and practitioners who are involved in research studies or engaged in using the results of such studies will find some of the issues in this report to be relevant to their work.

STRATEGIC OBJECTIVES

Across the topic areas addressed in the workshop series, we identified three strategic objectives for advancing scientific research in education:

1. promoting quality,
2. building the knowledge base, and
3. enhancing professional development.

Thus, the recommendations in this report have been organized to align with these strategies. Although some workshops track closely with these areas (for example, the workshop on doctoral programs in schools of education addresses professional development more so than the other areas), many cut across them.

A central idea that runs throughout the recommendations is that the diversity of the people in the field—with respect to the range of scholarly perspectives, training and background, and such demographic and social characteristics as race, ethnicity, gender, and age—can be very powerful if it rests on a common foundation. Diversity can promote quality, enhance legitimacy, and extend opportunity, but without reference to a common core, it can lead to fragmentation. Standardization without the flexibility to accommodate varying points of view leads to stultification. We seek to harness and extend the diversity of the field, while calling for attention to defining and reinforcing a common professional culture. One cannot exist without the other, and our recommendations are designed to reflect that premise.

A second and related idea throughout our analysis and recommendations is the importance of an active field of peers working to develop and to reinforce a professional culture. Whether through peer review processes in vetting proposals for research funding or manuscripts for publication, doctoral training, or informal communications and relationships, it is the participation of researchers in activities that strengthen the field as a whole that will advance scientific research in education. By recognizing common goals and working together to achieve them, there is great potential to further the field.

2

Promoting Quality

Rigorous studies of how students learn, how schools function, how teachers teach, and how the different cultural, political, economic, and demographic contexts in which these and related investigations are framed can provide (and have—see National Research Council, 2002, for examples) important insights into policy and practice. And yet poor research is in many ways worse than no research at all, because it is wasteful and promotes flawed models for effective knowledge generation. High-quality research is essential.

As described in Chapter 1, the questions of what constitutes high-quality education research and to what extent current scholarship meets those standards has taken on a high profile. Indeed, there is no shortage of answers. It is beyond the scope of this report to provide a fair and comprehensive description of the many important issues that have been raised in recent years with respect to how to define quality in scientific education research, or to comment on how the committee views them. Rather, in this chapter we begin with a brief discussion of how we define quality, taking our cue from *Scientific Research in Education,* and provide illustrations of select elements of quality that emerged in the committee's workshops. This cursory treatment of definitional issues is intended to provide the context for consideration of specific mechanisms for promoting high-quality scientific research in education.

ELEMENTS OF QUALITY

Scientific Research in Education was an attempt to articulate what is meant by quality with respect to scientific research in education. That book offered six principles that underlie all fields of scientific endeavor, including scientific research in education (National Research Council, 2002, p. 52):

1. Pose significant questions that can be investigated empirically.
2. Link research to relevant theory.
3. Use methods that permit direct investigation of the question.
4. Provide a coherent and explicit chain of reasoning.
5. Replicate and generalize across studies.
6. Disclose research to encourage professional scrutiny and critique.

In the scientific study of education, several features of teaching, learning, and schooling shape the ways in which the guiding principles are instantiated (e.g., the mobility of the student population). Together, the principles and the features provide a framework for thinking about the quality of scientific education research. We adopt this framework as our working definition of quality.

Recently, much attention has been focused on the methods used in education studies (most closely related to the third principle above), with a particular emphasis on randomized field trials to help establish cause-and-effect relationships (see, e.g., U.S. Department of Education, 2002, 2004; What Works Clearinghouse, 2004). Methods are the tools that researchers use to conduct their work; their appropriate use is essential to promoting quality.

Scientific Research in Education makes a number of important arguments related to methods. Specifically, the choice of method or methods must be driven by the question posed for investigation: no method can be judged as good, bad, scientific, or otherwise without reference to the question it is being used to address. In addition, scientific inferences are strengthened if they hold up under scrutiny through testing using multiple methods. A related and final point made in the book is that both quantitative and qualitative methods are needed to fully explore the range of questions about educational phenomena that are ripe for scientific study. The tendency in the current debates—in research, policy, and practice communities—to align with either quantitative or qualitative approaches is therefore neither sensible nor constructive. Indeed, working to integrate the two types of methods is likely to accelerate scientific progress.

Although these and related points about methodology are essential to understanding and promoting high-quality scientific research in education, an important conclusion of *Scientific Research in Education* is that scientific quality is a function of all six of these principles. Thus, in our view the national conversation about methodological quality is but the beginning of a broader dialogue that is necessary to fully address issues of scientific quality in education research. Here we provide a few examples of how discussions at the workshops illustrate the importance of other principles. While not exhaustive, they suffice to make the point that understanding and promoting high-quality scientific research in education requires attention to *all* principles.

- *Pose significant questions that can be investigated empirically.* A key idea embedded in this principle is that research questions should address important issues of practice, policy, and processes. During the peer review workshop, for example, participants highlighted the importance of ensuring that diverse groups of stakeholders be involved in developing federal agencies' research agendas, prioritizing research questions, and conducting the actual research. Without a range of scholarly perspectives and individuals traditionally underrepresented in education research, the types of questions addressed in a research portfolio will be necessarily limited in scope and are unlikely to hone in on significant questions across the broad swath of issues and populations in education.

- *Link research to relevant theory.* The workshop on building a knowledge base in education highlighted the critical role of theoretical constructs in research. Several workshop speakers discussed the process of relating data to a conceptual framework as guiding research and providing the support for scientific inference. Data enable assessments of the explanatory power of theoretical frameworks for modeling real-world phenomena; similarly, theories provide meaning for data. In Appendix B, we summarize an example from cross-cultural psychology and sociolinguistics that traces how related lines of inquiry developed as researchers moved back and forth between periods of empirical investigation and theory building, building on each other over time.

- *Replicate and generalize across studies.* The workshop on building an accumulated knowledge base in education also brought into sharp relief the core ideas of replication and generalization in science. No study is an island unto itself: scientific progress is achieved when results from multiple studies are interpreted jointly and the generalizability of theoretical concepts explored and articulated. Replication involves both application of the same conditions to multiple cases and replication of the designs, including cases that are sufficiently different to justify the generalization of results in theories. Without convergence of results from multiple studies, the objectivity, neutrality, and generalizability of research is questionable (Schneider, 2003). Appendix B includes more detail on these ideas.

MECHANISMS FOR PROMOTING QUALITY

There is no centralized place that ensures quality control in education research or any other scientific endeavor. Quality standards are often informal and their enforcement upheld by the norms and practices of the community of researchers (National Research Council, 2002). The diverse and diffuse nature of the investigators in the field of education research make common standards elusive; however, the workshops highlighted three leverage points for actively promoting high-quality research: peer review processes within federal agencies, implementation of research designs in educational settings, and partnerships between education research and practitioners.

Recommendation 1: In federal agencies that support education research, the criteria by which peer reviewers rate proposals should be clearly delineated, and the meaning of different score levels on each scale should be defined and illustrated. Reviewers should be trained in the use of these scales.

Earlier this year, the committee issued a report titled *Strengthening Peer Review in Federal Agencies That Support Education Research* (National Research Council, 2004b). That report details our conclusions and recommendations regarding the peer review processes of federal funding agencies and includes suggestions, among other recommendations, for how these systems can promote high-quality education research. In this recommendation, we highlight a critical mechanism for identifying and supporting high-quality scientific research in education through peer review: defining clear standards for the review and ensuring reviewers are trained in their use.

The process of peer review, in which investigators judge the merits of proposed new work, offers a natural place to engage the field in the contested but crucial task of developing and applying high standards for evaluating the merits of proposed research. The federal agencies represented at our workshop[1] all used different evaluation criteria in their peer review processes. The extent to which the criteria were defined, as well as the nature and intensity of training for reviewers on how to apply those criteria, varied as well. Given differences in mission and other factors, it is reasonable to expect variation in review criteria; however, we recommend that attention be paid to ensuring that criteria are clearly defined and based on valid and reliable measures. We also recommend that the development of training materials and the implementation of tutorials for reviewers become standard operating procedure, and that high-quality descriptive feedback associated with scores and group discussion be provided to applicants.

Research shows low levels of consistency in initial ratings of proposals across peer reviewers (Cicchetti and Conn, 1976; Kemper, McCarthy, and Cicchetti, 1996; Daniel, 1993; Cicchetti, 1991; Cole and Cole, 1981). There is potential for significant improvement in the reliability of ratings across reviewers through careful training on the rating scale criteria and on the rating process itself. This finding is consistent with a large literature on job performance ratings (Woehr and Huffcutt, 1994; Zedeck and Cascio, 1982) indicating the importance of careful definition of scale "anchors" and training in the rating process. The training of reviewers should focus deeply on the criteria used to evaluate research by defining those criteria very clearly, and training people to use them reliably. If reviewers do not have a clear understanding of what the criteria are, they carry their own frame of reference as a defining point into the review process, resulting in lower reliability of peer review, whether for manuscripts submitted to professional journals or for research grant proposals submitted for funding (Cichetti, 2003).

Not only could training improve the consistency of initial ratings across reviewers on a panel, but it also could facilitate group discussion that leads to stronger consensus and reliability of group ratings. It can have the added benefit of improving the validity of the feedback provided to applicants by better aligning it with the specific evaluation criteria, both in terms of the particular scores given and the descriptions of a proposal's strengths and weaknesses.

---

[1]The workshop included officials and staff from the Department of Education, the National Science Foundation, the National Institutes of Health, and the Office of Naval Research.

BOX 2-1
Training Peer Reviewers to Improve Research Quality

Teresa Levitin of the National Institute on Drug Abuse presented an example of a training program developed by agency staff for their peer reviewers. In describing the program, Levitin said that much of the training provided to reviewers takes place at the front end of the process, and that staff must work to diagnose potential issues starting with the initial contact with reviewers through the final submissions of scores and written comments at the conclusion of the panel. The training is both formal and informal, and focuses on general principles and policies.

The program Levitin described is provided on-line in advance of the peer review meeting and takes about 10 minutes to complete. Key elements of this training include:

- Orientation to the role of the peer reviewers in the grant-finding process.
- Instructions for identifying potential conflicts of interest in applications.
- Factors to consider or to ignore in making technical merit ratings.
- Guidance for providing specific comments and feedback for applicants.
- Expectations for participation in the panel meeting itself.

Throughout the mini course there are short "quiz" questions that present scenarios and prompt reviewers to apply ideas from the

---

Training is important to ensure that reviewers understand how to approach the evaluation of proposals and how to assign specific ratings to each criterion. At the workshop, Teresa Levitin of the National Institute on Drug Abuse provided several useful ideas for how to illustrate key concepts to reviewers about the review criteria in a relatively short amount of time (see Box 2-1). To our knowledge, there are few such models from which to learn about effective training practices in the specific context of peer review of education research proposals in federal agencies. Our recommendation is that agencies place strong emphasis on developing, evaluating, and refining training programs to ensure that reviewers are applying criteria in ways

course to real-life situations that often arise in reviewing applications.

Levitin also described a process for monitoring reviewers, from start to finish, and taking action when needed to correct inaccurate or inappropriate comments. Monitoring begins with embedded questions in the training course and continues through analysis of the resulting ratings and feedback comments.

No assessment of the effectiveness of the training and monitoring program described by Levitin was presented at the workshop. The design of this program, however, is highly consistent with long-established findings from industrial psychology on effective ways to improve the reliability and validity of job performance ratings (Borman, 1979; Pulakos, 1986; Hauenstein, 1998). The course is available for viewing online at http://www7.nationalacademies.org/core/review_course_nih_version.pdf.

Workshop:	Peer Review of Education Research Grant Applications Implications, Considerations, and Future Directions February 25-26, 2003 Transcript available at: http://www7.nationalacademies.org/core/
Key Speaker:	Teresa Levitin, National Institute on Drug Abuse
Related Product:	*Strengthening Peer Review in Federal Agencies That Support Education Research* http://books.nap.edu/catalog/1054.html

that are intended, contributing to the process in effective ways, and learning from the experience.

Delivering feedback to applicants can also be an effective way to signal the field's (often implicit) standards of quality, reinforcing them in a formal context. Indeed, one workshop participant argued that "peer review is not just about judging scientific merit, it is about defining it and creating it" (Redish, 2003).

Finally, the role of peer reviewers is typically to provide advice to the head of the agency about the relative merits of proposals they considered— usually in the form of a slate of ranked proposals. The decision makers in these agencies must be responsive to the results of the peer review process, yet they do play a role in ensuring quality in what they choose to fund based on that advice. It could well be that few proposals submitted in a particular competition will lead to research of the highest quality. In this case, the most important way to improve the quality of education research is to fund those few and then have appropriate agency staff work with unsuccessful applicants to improve the quality of their future proposals. Such decisions can be politically risky—if appropriators see that funds have not been spent at year's end, they very well may decide to cut funding levels in the next fiscal year. Effectively balancing these very real potential consequences against quality concerns will take courage and leadership at the highest ranks of the agency.

Quality standards used to vet manuscripts for publication by peer-reviewed journals are similarly important. They are likely to be different from those used in the peer review of proposals because the products (manuscripts rather than proposals) are different. To some degree, standards will vary because each journal has its own niche in the scholarly community. A roundtable of editors and other participants in manuscript review and publication featured at one of the workshops made this clear: some journals are primarily theory-based; others exclusively empirical. Some are archival; others publish syntheses of related work over a period of time. In addition, reviewers of manuscripts submitted for publication in a journal rarely interact to discuss the strengths and weaknesses of submissions. Nonetheless, explicit attention to standards for manuscript review, along the same lines as for proposal review, is essential for promoting high-quality education research.

> **Recommendation 2: Federal agencies that support education research should ensure that as a group, each peer review panel has the research experience and expertise to judge the theoretical and technical merits of the proposals it reviews. In addition, peer review panels should be composed so as to minimize conflicts of interest, to balance biases, and to promote the participation of people from a range of scholarly perspectives and traditionally underrepresented groups.**

Deciding who counts as a peer is central to quality considerations: the peer review process, no matter how well designed, is only as good as the people involved. Judging the competence of peers in any research field is a complex task requiring assessment on a number of levels. In education research, it is particularly difficult because the field is so diverse (e.g., with respect to disciplinary training and background, epistemological orientation) and diffuse (e.g., housed in various university departments and research institutions, working on a wide range of education problems and issues). The workshop discussions brought out several related issues and illustrated the difficulties in, and disagreements associated with, assembling the right people for the job.

The first priority for assembling a peer review panel is to ensure that it encompasses the research experience and expertise necessary to evaluate the theoretical and technical aspects of the proposals to be reviewed. For agencies that fund education research, we define "theoretical and technical aspects" to refer to three areas: (1) the substance or topics of the proposals, (2) the research methods proposed, and (3) the educational practice or policy contexts in which the proposal is situated. Relevant experience and expertise should be determined broadly, based on the range of proposal types and program priorities. If, for example, a specialized quantitative research design is being proposed, at least some of the reviewers should have expertise in this design; if a specialized qualitative research design is proposed, some reviewers should have expertise in this design.

In addition, it is the range of proposal types and program priorities, not their frequency or conventionality, that should determine the scope of the panel's experience and expertise. In most cases, individual panelists will have relevant experience and expertise in one or more, but not all, of the topics and techniques under review. It is the distributed expertise of the review panel as a whole, and not the individual members, that establishes the appropriateness of the panel for the task (Hackett and Chubin, 2003). In this way, peer review is "intended to free [decision making] from the domination of any particular individual's preferences, making it answerable to the peer community as a whole, within the discipline or specialty" (Harnad, 1998, p. 110).

Reviewers should not harbor biases against other researchers or forms of research, nor should they have conflicts of interest that arise from the possibility of gaining or losing professionally or financially from the work under review (e.g., they work at the same institution). It is critical that reviewers can be counted on to judge research proposals on merit. But in practice, it is not possible to avoid researchers in the same field knowing one another's work and each other personally. They may have biases for or against a certain type of research. They may be competitors for the same research dollars or the same important discovery or have other conflicts of interest associated with the research team proposed in a study (e.g., a past student-faculty adviser relationship). In such situations, impartiality is easily compromised and partiality not always acknowledged (Eisenhart, 2002). However, Chubin and Hackett (1990) argue that increases in specialization and interdisciplinary research have shrunk the pool of qualified reviewers to the point at which only those with a conflict of interest are truly qualified to conduct the review. Potential conflicts of interest must be minimized, and biases balanced. Both are serious limitations of peer review and can probably be addressed in the long term only by expanding the pools of qualified reviewers, through training and outreach to experts traditionally underrepresented in the process.

In assembling peer review panels, attention to the diversity of potential reviewers with respect to disciplinary orientation as well as social background characteristics also is important to promote quality. Peer review panels made up of experts who come from different fields and disciplines and who rely on different methodological tools can together promote a technically strong, relevant research portfolio that builds and extends on that diversity of perspectives. Similarly, diverse panels with respect to salient social characteristics of researchers can be an effective tool for grounding the review in the contexts in which the work is done and for promoting research that is relevant to, and appropriate for, a broad range of educational issues and student populations.

There is a final and particularly contentious issue related to diversity and to identifying the peers to review proposals for education research: how education practitioners and community members should be involved. Because education research is applied and attention to the relevance of the work is crucial, it is essential to involve practitioners and community members in the work of the agency. Whether and how they participate on panels, however, is a difficult question. A major concern with the practice of including reviewers without research expertise is that it could lead to inadequate reviews with respect to criteria of technical merit (or, in the criteria we defined above, research methods), a critical aspect of research proposal review in all agencies.[2] In addition, since the field of education research is

---

[2]We recognize that some practitioners and community members do have research expertise. In these cases, the concerns we outline do not apply. Our focus here is on those practitioners and community members who do not bring this expertise to peer review deliberations.

in the early stages of developing scientific norms for peer review, this important process could be complicated or slowed by the participation of individuals who do not have a background in research.

We do see the potential benefits of including practitioners and community members on panels that are evaluating education research funding applications, identifying high-quality proposals, and contributing to professional development opportunities for researchers, practitioners, and community members alike. Thus, we conclude that this option is one of four possible strategies—including reviewing proposals alongside researchers, reviewing proposals after researchers' reviews, serving on priority-setting or policy boards, or participating in retrospective reviews of agency portfolios—that agencies could adopt to actively engage practitioner and community member groups in their work.

A final note: while our focus is on federal funding agencies, this recommendation on peer review of proposals for education research is applicable to similar foundation efforts. Much education research is supported by private and not-for-profit organizations, and their role in promoting high-quality research through their grant-making is a significant one.

Similarly, journals, through their choice of editors, publication committee members, and reviewers, as well as their manuscript review procedures, perform a significant role in shaping the quality of scholarly work. Just as funding agencies that screen proposals need to ensure a highly qualified, diverse set of reviewers, so too must the publication outlets that publish the finished research products.

Recommendation 3: In research conducted in educational settings, investigators must not only select rigorous methods appropriate to the questions posed but also implement them in ways that meet the highest standards of evidence for those questions and methods.

As described above, a critical scientific principle is the idea that the choice of methods used in particular studies should be driven by the nature of the question being investigated. This notion was extended in the workshop on the conduct of one method—randomized field trials—in educational settings to focus attention on the importance of rigorous implementation of research methods in educational settings. The report *Implementing Randomized Field Trials in Education: Report of a Workshop* contains a full accounting of the many practical issues associated with successful research of this kind discussed at the event (National Research Council, 2004a).

Randomized field trials in education, when they are feasible and ethical, are highly effective methods for gauging the effects of interventions on educational outcomes (National Research Council, 2002). The power of random assignment of students (or schools, or other unit of study) to groups is that, on average, the two groups that result are initially the same, differing only in terms of the intervention.[3] This allows researchers to more confidently attribute differences they observe between the two groups to the intervention, rather than to the known and unknown other factors that influence human behavior and performance. As in any comparative study, researchers must be careful to observe and account for any other confounding variables that could differentially affect the groups after randomization has taken place. That is, even though randomization creates (statistically) equivalent groups at the outset, once the intervention is under way, other events or programs could take place in one group and not the other, undermining any attempt to isolate the effect of the intervention. Furthermore, the use of multiple methods in such studies is highly desirable: for example, observational techniques can depict the implementation of the intervention and sharpen the ability to understand and isolate the influence it has on outcomes.

The primary focus of the workshop was on how this kind of design can be implemented successfully in district or school settings. Pairs of researcher-practitioner teams described their experiences designing and conducting randomized field trials in schools in Baltimore and suburban Pittsburgh and made clear that the selection of this method is not sufficient to ensuring that a rigorous study is conducted—implementation matters. The challenges they described are daunting. Recruitment and retention of students and schools to participate are fraught with difficulties associated with trust, mobility and turnover of student and teacher populations, and laborious consent processes. Teachers are likely to share ideas and practices that seem promising, blurring differences between the interventions the two

---

[3]It is logically possible that differences between the groups may still be due to idiosyncratic differences between individuals assigned to each group. However, with randomization, the chances of this occurring (a) can be explicitly calculated and (b) can be made very small, typically by a straightforward manipulation like increasing the number of individuals assigned to each group.

groups receive. Life intervenes: in the studies described at the workshop, research tasks were affected by a fatal fire, a snowstorm, and a government shutdown.

The presenters offered ways of anticipating and dealing with many of these problems, all of which were facilitated by the development of strong partnerships between the research team and district and school personnel. Some strategies for overcoming obstacles involve design features: for example, the so-called Power4Kids study recently launched in a consortium of districts outside of Pittsburgh was designed to address the concern that the process of random assignment may result in some students not receiving a promising intervention. Each of the participating schools was assigned to test one of four reading tutorials, so the study design does not exclude any school from these interventions (students were then randomly assigned within each school to an intervention or to continue to receive existing instruction) (Myers, 2003). Other strategies involve facilitating key implementation tasks, like training school-based personnel to coordinate obtaining consent from participants and to monitor compliance with random assignment to groups. Without the mutual trust and understanding that is enabled by a strong partnership, none of these strategies is feasible. Furthermore, expertise and flexibility in research staff and adequate project resources are needed to deal successfully with unforeseen issues as they arise (Gueron, 2003).

In our view, the importance of attending to proper planning and implementation of design features is just as important for other kinds of methods when doing work in real-world educational settings. The workshop series did not address implementation issues with other methods directly (e.g., surveys, ethnographic studies), but explicit attention to them is important as a focus of future work.

Recommendation 4: Federal agencies should ensure appropriate resources are available for education researchers conducting large-scale investigations in educational settings to build partnerships with practitioners and policy makers.

As we have argued above, a key lesson that emerged from the workshop on implementing randomized field trials in education is that the quality of any large-scale research conducted in districts or schools—largely independent of method or design—depends significantly on relationships built between researchers and district- and school-based personnel.

Educators are often wary of researchers. The reasons for this uneasiness, both perceived and real, are many: educators may feel that the topics of study do not align with the concerns they face from day to day, research tasks require their scarce time and effort to accommodate, and many kinds of research require that educators cede control of instructional decision making to investigators to meet research goals.

Workshop discussions made clear that these circumstances have significant bearing on research quality. Without addressing them directly and working toward commonly held goals, educators have little incentive to ensure that research protocols are followed; to recognize, prevent, or communicate problems or issues relevant to the study's objectives that arise during the study period (e.g., treatment fidelity issues in comparative studies); or to bring their observations and insights to bear on the research. Partnerships, especially those that are sensitive to issues of racial and ethnic diversity and bridging gaps in ethnicity and socioeconomic status that often exist between researchers and those in the districts and schools, enhance the ability to address these issues.

In each of the three studies featured at the workshop, researchers were able to gain access to the schools, to ensure cooperation in faithfully carrying out the interventions, and to make progress toward mutual goals by establishing trust and encouraging open communication. Their experiences suggest that it is nearly impossible for researchers to conduct randomized field trials—or any other large-scale study—in districts and schools unless both researchers and education service providers take time to understand each others' goals and develop a study design that will help both parties to reach them. The committee was particularly impressed with one model for how researcher-practitioner partnerships can be developed and nurtured to change these incentives to the advantage of all. This two-decade-old partnership in the Baltimore City Public School System that promotes research and practice simultaneously in the context of a series of randomized field trials is described in Box 2-2.

Over the past four years, the National Research Council has issued a series of reports focused on how such partnerships could form the basis of a major new education research infrastructure called the Strategic Education Research Partnership (SERP). The culminating proposal (National Research Council, 2003b) contains many of the elements of a partnership described in Box 2-2. Indeed, part of the justification for the large-scale effort is that there are many such examples of productive partnerships (involving randomized field trials and other kinds of education research), but they are not connected in a way that contributes to a unified body of knowledge or that improve practice on a large scale. One of the three main components of the SERP plan is field sites, which are built on the kinds of tenets featured in the partnerships described at the workshop: mutual trust, collaborative prioritization, and deployment of resources to support the research-practice partnership.

Creating these partnerships requires time and money. To implement the model for the series of large-scale randomized field trials described in Box 2-2, for example, the researcher-practitioner team estimate the need for a year of work *before* the research is formally launched. Thus, when funding large-scale studies to be conducted in educational settings, federal agencies and other funders need to ensure that adequate resources are available for partnership building. And investigators need to take the task seriously and spend the time in advance establishing that understanding and trust.

Of course, not all education research requires working relationships with districts or schools. For example, education policy research that focuses on macro-level trends and relationships typically involves the use of existing large-scale data sets. However, even these kinds of projects rely (albeit less directly) on the fact that someone had to engage schools or districts or other educational settings to gather the data. Furthermore, appropriate interpretations of information that was collected may be difficult without thorough grounding in the context of the classroom. The bottom line is that promoting high-quality education research requires consideration of how to effectively engage districts and schools, and this requires time and money in research budgets, regardless of the study design.

CONCLUSION

The field of education research and the related goals of evidence-based education will not be served if the underlying science lacks rigor. In this chapter we point to ways in which quality can be promoted in a range of settings. Overall, the approach taps different institutions and thus the talents and energies of a wide range of practicing scholars in the field. Acting on these recommendations, therefore, could formally engage a broad swath of the diverse talent of education researchers and enrich the ongoing dialogues about quality in turn.

BOX 2-2
Effective Implementation of Education Research
Through Partnerships

The Kellam-Chinnia team described a series of randomized studies in the Baltimore City schools that have stretched over two decades in the context of the larger, long-term Baltimore Prevention Program that have been supported by a strong partnership between the research team and district- and school-based personnel. The current study is exploring the effects of an integrated set of preventive first-grade interventions aimed at improving teachers' classroom behavior management, family-classroom partnerships regarding homework and discipline, and teachers' instructional practices regarding academic subjects, particularly reading.

Chinnia explained that the school system supports the study because it lays the foundation for translating its findings into policy and practice. In addition to assessing the impact of the program, the researchers will follow the first-grade children as far as the end of third grade, and they will also follow their first-grade teachers over two subsequent cohorts of first graders. This long-term observation will allow researchers to test whether the multiple levels of support and training for teachers sustain high levels of program practice. The study will also test in the fourth year whether the support and training structure is successful in training nonprogram teachers.

In their presentation, Kellam and Chinnia described how their partnership helped both the education community and the research team meet their goals. Kellam asserted that when a partnership is in place based on "mutual self-interests at multiple levels," obtaining the consent of the parents of participating children requires far less logistical work than otherwise might be the case—illustrating how key implementation tasks such as recruitment are facilitated by the relationship. Chinnia described some of the self-interests that led to the long-term partnership. She explained that the randomized field trials helped to meet several of the school system's goals, including intervening early in elementary school to enhance and maintain student achievement, identifying best practices for instruction and classroom management, and promoting parent involvement in students' progress. She noted that the current study could help to sustain best practices in a whole-day first-grade program, and that the goal of creating and sustaining whole-day first grade programs is included in the Baltimore City Public School System's master plan.

In sum, they described the development of an effective partnership as requiring six essential components (Kellam, 2000, p. 19):

1. Analyze the social/political structure of the school district.
2. Learn the vision and understand the challenges and priorities.
3. Identify mutual self-interests within and across the leadership.
4. Fit the prevention research/program interests under the visions of the leadership.
5. Request ad hoc oversight committee of leaders.
6. Work through trust issues.

Workshop:	Randomized Field Trials in Education: Implementation and Implications September 24, 2003 Transcript available at: http://www7.nationalacademies.org/core/
Key Speakers:	Sheppard Kellam, American Institutes for Research Linda Chinnia, Baltimore City Public School System
Related Product:	*Implementing Randomized Field Trials in Education: Report of a Workshop* http://books.nap.edu/catalog/10943.html

3

Building the Knowledge Base

Even if the quality of discrete education research studies is outstanding, if the field is not able to forge connections among them, it will amass a multitude of studies that cannot support inferences about the generalizability of findings nor sustain the long-term theory building that drives scientific progress. Forging connections among studies will enable the field to be more than the sum of its parts. Lacking the infrastructure or the professional norms to engage in efforts to connect and integrate theories and data across investigations, the scientific study of educational phenomena will be fragmented (as some currently are; see Lagemann, 2000). The progression of scientific knowledge in education (and other scientific fields) is neither linear nor predictable, but it can be facilitated by explicit efforts to promote the accumulation of research-based knowledge.

FRAMING CONCEPTS

Two of our five workshops had considerable bearing on the committee's deliberations on this topic. The first of these workshops was designed to consider a range of strategies that might foster the growth of a cumulative knowledge base in education, including the development of common measures of key constructs, data sharing and replication, and ways of taking stock of what has been learned. During this first workshop, scholars from a range of fields also explored how the nature of scientific knowledge itself influences knowledge building. An understanding of the core nature of education research and how it is similar and different from other fields and disciplines is an important foundation for the recommendations in this chapter. An analysis of some of conceptual ideas discussed at this workshop—such as the relationship of education research to educational practice, the context dependence of findings, and its public character—is presented in Appendix B. Extending this wide-ranging day-and-a-half of dialogue, a second workshop examined in greater depth the role of education research journals in both promoting high-quality and a more integrated knowledge base.

A passage from *Scientific Research in Education* helps to clarify how we view the idea of knowledge accumulation by linking the key concepts of theory and generalizability: "It is the long-term goal of much of science to generate theories that can offer stable explanations for phenomena that generalize beyond the particular. . . . Science generates cumulative knowledge by building on, refining, and occasionally replacing, theoretical understanding" (National Research Council, 2002, p. 3).

Theoretical constructs provide an organizing conception to which research inquiries relate, creating a common point of reference that can facilitate efforts to make sense of the wide diversity of studies and findings in education research. They give meaning to data, drive the selection of questions and methods, and provide the foundation for large-scale data collection efforts. For example, in the National Assessment of Educational Progress, designing the noncognitive data collection (that is, background data on test-takers, schools, teachers, and instruction) around a coherent set of strong theories would result in a more streamlined data set and promote more coherent lines of investigations focused on well-articulated theoretical models (Grissmer, 2003).

Theory also drives replications, a powerful tool for establishing generalizaiblity. Replicating an investigation with comparable subjects and conditions to see if similar results are achieved is essential for being able to generalize to more people and settings than are represented in a single study (Shadish, Cook, and Campbell, 2002; Cronbach et al., 1980; Cronbach, 1982) and to clarify the boundaries of prevailing theories. Replication involves applying the same conditions to multiple cases, as well as replicating the design and including cases that are sufficiently different to justify the generalization of results and theories.

In many of the natural and physical sciences, there are professional norms that encourage data sharing—a practice that enables verifications and replications and provides opportunities for investigating new questions, forging interdisciplinary links, and developing and validating measures. In addition, there are multiple experiments focused on the same issue from different perspectives. New technology has allowed changes in how research is conducted in these fields. For example, in modern astronomy, natural observation has been transformed through the collection and processing of images of phenomena—images and information that are available to multiple investigators simultaneously (Knorr-Cetina, 1999). Consortiums of scientists work on data sets housed in centralized databases. Similarly, in physics, there are projects in which researchers, linked through various technologies, work on problems at the same time in locations throughout the world, searching for new phenomena.

Working with data on solar systems is different from working with data on human beings. Research involving humans brings with it fundamental moral and legal responsibilities to protect their rights. These protections shape, and sometimes constrain, data collection, data sharing, and data use.[1] For this and other reasons, education researchers rarely replicate their work or that of their peers or reanalyze the findings of others using secondary data. But it is important to recognize that research is not a covert activity, and individual investigators have a professional obligation to contribute to the advancement of their field. For example, when secondary analyses of large-scale databases and data collections have been conducted, they have proven fruitful; see Box 3-1 for an example that shows the value of secondary analysis of existing data. And maximizing data sharing while ensuring the confidentiality of research participants—topics we take up in some detail in the next section—is yet another way in which the field can work collaboratively to advance scientific understanding and progress.

MECHANISMS FOR BUILDING THE KNOWLEDGE BASE

We see three points of leverage for encouraging knowledge accumulation in education research: professional associations, scholarly journals, and infrastructure supports like data banks. Efforts like data sharing should be supported by professional norms that are developed through sanctions and rewards and reinforced informally by the community of researchers

---

[1]Many of the other barriers to data sharing, however, are common among all sciences (National Research Council, 1985).

(Schneider, 2003). The recommendations in this chapter target these leverage points and call for formal efforts to encourage knowledge accumulation in education research. They serve to focus attention on the development of theories and explicit attempts to reanalyze, replicate, and test the boundaries of those theories with empirical inquiries. Although we focus on institutions in the recommendations, it is critical to acknowledge that all members of the education research communities need to be involved in contributing to and using these infrastructure supports. The tools themselves will not promote the broader goal of scientific progress; their active and effective use by the field will. A recent National Research Council committee captures this idea in discussing publication and data sharing in particular (2003a, p. 4):

> Community standards for sharing publication-related data and materials should flow from the general principle that the publication of scientific information is intended to move science forward. More specifically, the act of publishing is a *quid pro quo* in which authors receive credit and acknowledgment in exchange for disclosure of their scientific findings. An author's obligation is not only to release data and materials to enable others to verify or replicate published findings . . . but also to provide them in a form on which other scientists can build with further research. All members of the scientific community—whether working in academia, government, or a commercial enterprise—have equal responsibility for upholding community standards as participants in the publication system, and all should be equally able to derive benefits from it.

It is in this spirit that the committee makes the following recommendations.

Recommendation 5: Professional associations involved in education research should develop explicit ethical standards for data sharing.

Data are the foundation of scientific inquiry, and sharing them among peers is one direct way to facilitate the transparency, accountability, and scholarly communication so vital to scientific advancement (National Research Council, 2002). Sharing data among investigators working on common areas of inquiry enables the production of knowledge that can only be derived from merging, comparing, combining, reanalyzing, or integrating data. Indeed, the potential benefits of data sharing are many, because the practice enables the direct interplay between data and theory at every stage of development in a line of inquiry. In education research, data sharing can

BOX 3-1
The Value of Data Sharing

In describing his experience gaining access to and using the infamous Coleman data, workshop speaker Ron Ehrenberg provided a vivid example of the importance of data sharing in education research, as well as the need to prepare adequate documentation of data to enable further analyses. In the early 1990s, Ehrenberg and his colleague Dominic Brewer became interested in the effects on student achievement of school districts' efforts to aggressively increase their hiring of underrepresented minority faculty. The underlying assumption of these efforts was that minority teachers would be more effective teachers of minority students because they could serve as role models, had higher expectations for these students, and would provide more positive feedback to them. In order to accomplish their hiring objectives, many school districts were providing financial incentives for their older, experienced teachers to retire, even in the face of a declining pool of minorities seeking to enter careers in education and evidence that new minority teachers were under-performing on teacher certification exams compared with new white teachers. Ehrenberg and Brewer wanted to test the results of trading off teacher experience, educational preparation, and academic ability for teacher race and ethnicity on both minority and non-minority students.

The ideal data set for this purpose would contain information on teacher and student characteristics, including teachers' educational background, test scores, and experience. The data would be individual in nature so that students could be matched to specific teachers, and they would be longitudinal in order to permit examination of the relationship between students' test scores and teacher characteristics during the time period.

While no individual-level data sets from a contemporary period provided the information required for the analysis, Ehrenberg and Brewer determined that they could use the school-level data from the Equal Opportunity Survey (EOS) database (the data on which the 1966 Coleman report, *On Equality of Educational Opportunity*, was based) if they were willing to make one crucial assumption; because these data were not longitudinal in nature, they needed to assume that differences in test score performance between two grades in a school at a point in time were reasonable proxies for how much students would learn if they remained at the school for both grades. Despite such limitations, Ehrenberg and Brewer wanted to use an existing data set rather than engage in an original data collection effort due to the immediacy of the question.

The EOS data are considered one of the most important social science data sets of their era. However, Ehrenberg reported that these data are not well archived—the data he received from the National Archives were poorly documented, and data records were missing entirely for more than 5,800 of the original 50,000 teachers surveyed. As a result, he had to overcome several methodological issues in order to conduct his analysis. Ehrenberg's and Brewer's (1995) findings included evidence that teacher's academic ability correlated with higher student achievement, and that a higher percentage of black teachers in a school correlated with greater academic achievement for black students but lower achievement for white students. Recognizing that these findings had considerable policy implications, Ehrenberg and Brewer cautioned that policy decisions should not be made based on evidence from one study alone. Indeed, they subsequently used data from the National Education Longitudinal Study of 1988 (NELS) to re-examine their research question (Ehrenberg, Goldhaber, and Brewer, 1995). As with the EOS data, the NELS data were not perfectly suited to their analysis, but they provided several advantages over the EOS data. Although they did not include measures of teacher academic ability, they came from a more contemporary period, permitting Ehrenberg and Brewer to extend their analysis to consider the matching of teachers and students not only by race but also by gender and ethnicity. They found that, for the most part, the match of teachers and students by race, gender, and ethnicity did not affect how much students learned. However, they did find evidence that racial matching sometimes influenced teachers' subjective evaluations of students, which might in turn influence students' aspirations and the tracks on which they are put.

While the findings from these data sets are not entirely consistent, Ehrenberg argued, there is enough commonality to suggest the need to train teachers to be effective with all population groups, regardless of race or ethnicity. Without the availability of these data sets and techniques for adapting data to new questions, this research would not have been possible in such a timely fashion.

Workshop: Understanding and Promoting Knowledge Accumulation in Education Research: Tools and Strategies
June 30-July 1, 2003
Transcript available at: http://www7.nationalacademies.org/core/

Key Speaker: Ronald Ehrenberg, Cornell University

facilitate the verification of results obtained by allowing other researchers to reproduce them, enable replications that test the boundaries of theories and help articulate their generalizability, promote the development of validated measures, and provide opportunities (and often cost savings) to pursue new questions and directions. Thus, sharing data can facilitate growth in new areas of inquiry by allowing groups of researchers to consider how others' data, measures, and constructs reinforce, call into question, extend, or refute their own, enabling collaborative thinking and advances in investigating phenomena—such as learning processes—that require in-depth contextual analysis and differentiation.

One mechanism for encouraging and facilitating data-sharing and knowledge accumulation is the development of ethical standards for data sharing in the professional and scientific associations that represent education researchers and related social scientists (and reinforcement of those standards in the publishing policies of their journals; see Recommendation 6). The American Psychological Association (APA), the American Anthropological Association (AAA), and the American Sociological Association (ASA), all have such standards; they vary in strength but encourage the same concept. For example, one part of the ASA code reads: "Sociologists make their data available after completion of the project or its major publications, except where proprietary agreements with employers, contractors or clients preclude such accessibility" (American Sociological Association, 1999, p. 16). And a part of the AAA code states: "The AAA supports the sharing of research data and encourages ethnographers to consider preserving field notes, tapes, videos, etc. as a resource accessible to others for future study. Ethnographers should inform participants of the intent to preserve the data and make it accessible as well as the precautions to be undertaken in the handling of the data" (American Anthropological Association, 2004).

Notably, however, the last revision to the ethics code at the American Educational Research Association (AERA) was in 2000, and it did not result in the addition of such data-sharing elements. We urge the AERA to adopt such a standard, and we encourage other such associations to continue to revisit their standards to promote the maximum ethical use of data.

How to craft and implement such a policy in a way that protects the fundamental right to information privacy is a matter of some complexity (National Research Council, 2000). Any data-sharing policy must ensure that privacy and confidentiality safeguards are in place to protect data on study participants and groups of participants; that the rights of, and protections for, authors are considered; and that standards are appropriate for the different types of research conducted under the umbrella of education research.

A host of federal laws and regulations govern the collection of education data in relation to privacy and confidentiality issues. Key privacy laws include those that govern all research involving human participants (e.g., the Privacy Act of 1974) and those pertaining to education research involving human participants in particular (e.g., the Protection of Pupil Rights Act and the Federal Educational Rights and Privacy Act). Additionally, the Education Sciences Reform Act governs confidentiality issues in education research, and the so-called "common rule" from the code of federal regulations (CFR, Title 45, part 5) provides a regulatory framework for the protection of human participants in education and other fields. Each of these statutes and regulations affects the collection of data from human research participants in education research, and therefore are likely to apply to the sharing of data for further analysis as well.

Ensuring compliance with federal laws and regulations governing human research participant protections and safeguards is mainly the responsibility of institutional review boards (IRB). Every institution has its own IRB. Every IRB has its own policy on data collections and data sharing, and no single interpretation or set of guidelines has emerged. The historical focus of IRBs on informed consent and notification policies to protect the rights of human research participants is complex and widely variable (National Research Council, 2000), and their experience considering and encouraging data sharing while protecting these rights limited. These complexities notwithstanding, there are IRBs that recognize and promote the ethical sharing of data that can be used as models to facilitate its practice more broadly (see, e.g., University of Pittsburgh IRB Manual).

Conceptually, maintaining confidentiality requires attention to three relevant questions: Who has access to data? What are threats to confidentiality? What are techniques for protecting confidentiality? (Bradburn, 2003). On the question of who has access to the data, typically there is a restricted set of people who have full access to data and have promised to protect the confidentiality of the subjects. A key question is how this "umbrella of confidentiality" can be extended while ensuring that the responsibilities of confidentiality are upheld. With respect to the second question, a common threat to confidentiality occurs any time a researcher adds data to an existing data set, because the addition of, for example, geographic information to a person file increases the potential to identify individuals and complicates efforts to maintain confidentiality. Another source of threats stems from law enforcement. The Patriot Act, for example, provides for government access to any individual data collected by a federal agency, even education statistics, with few exceptions, and data can be subpoenaed for various reasons (Bradburn, 2003). Finally, threats to maintaining confidentiality are typically more pronounced with the sharing of qualitative data. Developing strategies for maintaining confidentiality with such data will require broad and creative effort, but is just as important a goal to work toward as the sharing of quantitative data.

In promoting broader data sharing while ensuring privacy and confidentiality safeguards, the field can learn many valuable lessons from the experience of federal statistical agencies (e.g., the National Center for Education Statistics [NCES] and the U.S. Census Bureau) and work to adapt and extend them to different types of data. There are two main strategies for protecting confidentiality: restricting access and altering data (Bradburn, 2003).

For example, agencies may restrict access so that it is permitted only in data enclaves. This is the model used at the U.S. Census Bureau, which supports a number of research data centers around the country. There are very strict controls over access, but the centers permit a lot of research that would be otherwise impossible to conduct. Another model is used at NCES. Both public-use data files and restricted-use data files are available: the public-use files contain anonymous versions of individually identifiable data; restricted-use files contain more detailed, individually identifiable data, although direct identifiers such as Social Security numbers and addresses are removed from all analysis files. Access to public-use data is open to any interested party. Restricted-use files are available only to qualified researchers for approved statistical purposes. Researchers apply for a license and are loaned a data file, and their use of the file is subject to the terms of a license agreement.

A strategy of altering data can also be an effective way to maximize access to data while maintaining confidentiality of research participants. Ways of altering data include such strategies as holding identification data in a separate file, and creating synthetic data sets (Bradburn, 2003).

NCES currently has more than 100 public-use microdata files with data from the late 1980s through the present available on its web site. Data files from the 1960s and 1970s are also available through an archive. Researchers can manipulate the data in a number of these files using the NCES Data Analysis System. In addition, NCES has developed a set of tools to facilitate access to the data, including several on-line tools. It is possible to look up basic data on individual schools and to compare schools in a variety of ways, such as by having a similar characteristic (e.g., size; rural, suburban, or urban; etc.). NCES also provides a set of prerun tables that permit individuals to cut the tables in different directions, such as getting student scores by several different variables (Seastrom, 2003). These policies avail education researchers of opportunities to mine the extensive data sets collected by NCES, and do so in a way that protects the privacy and confidentiality of research participants.

Recommendation 6: Education research journals should require authors to make relevant data available to other researchers as a condition of publication and to ensure that applicable ethical standards are upheld.

Norms for data sharing in many of the physical and natural sciences are reinforced in their professional and disciplinary journals. In journals such as *Science* and *Nature*, once an article is published, the author has to make the data available to those who wish to replicate the results. In both of those publications, authors are required to provide their data arrayed in identified files that directly correspond to results reported in the tables and figures in the manuscript. The *Proceedings of the National Academy of Sciences* has a similar policy: the journal will also house the data if appropriate data repositories do not exist. If authors of published articles refuse to comply with requests for their data, the journal bars them from future publishing.

Similar traditions in the social and behavioral sciences and education journals are not as well established. There are exceptions, however. The *American Economic Review,* for example, has a policy similar to those in the *Nature* and *Science*. In addition, journals published by the APA require authors to provide the data relevant to their articles to competent researchers. There are problems implementing these sorts of policies, as well as issues associated with promoting replication and reanalysis even when such policies do exist. For example, although APA's data-sharing policy had been in effect for 25 years, staff estimates that less than one-tenth of a percent (0.001) of available data are actually shared as the policy envisions (VandenBos, 2003).

In our view, this low rate of use among psychologists reflects a host of cultural barriers and institutional incentives structures that work against data sharing that also exist in education research. Data sharing directly involves two parties: the person or organization that originally collected the data and the person or organization that would like to make use of an existing data source.[2] Disincentives exist for both (Natriello, 2003).

For individual researchers who have engaged in data collection, it is not always clear how to prepare data to share, a problem that has intensified as data sets have become more complex. A further disincentive along this line is that the process of preparing data to be shared requires considerable effort (and therefore cost) beyond what is required for preparing data for analysis and publication. A lack of standards for the preparation and archiving of public data sets leads to institutions and individuals having to reinvent the wheel in determining how to go about the process of data preparation. Finally, researchers may be reluctant to share their data because when they do so, they lose exclusivity for reporting on the data. Researchers often want to hold their data as long as possible so that they have the advantage in analyzing them before the larger community gains access to them (Natriello, 2003).

There are also disincentives for researchers who want to use existing data. Such efforts often require researchers to expend considerable effort (and therefore cost) in order to overcome technical barriers. Some researchers do not view the work as truly their own if they were not involved in the data collection. Finally, publication outlets can serve as a significant disincentive for conducting work using existing data. Peer-reviewed journals as well as tenure and promotion policies both tend to value publications that strike off in new directions or provide novel ideas and to devalue studies that build on previous work (Schneider, 2003; Natriello, 2003).

These and related issues will need to be addressed formally to mitigate such disincentives. For example, universities and departments could work to change tenure and promotion decisions so that they recognize efforts that promote data sharing as valuable intellectual contributions to the field; a singular focus on rewarding researchers for publishing in a small set of elite journals may not serve the field in the long run. Associations could lead an effort to develop standards and protocols for preparing data to be shared. And federal funding agencies could encourage the sharing of data by outlining the conditions under which it is permissible in the informa-

---

[2]Other parties have a role in, and may present conflicting interests with respect to, data-sharing (e.g., the public, federal funding agencies); see National Research Council (1985) for a discussion.

tion provided to its grantees. Individual education researchers can also facilitate these efforts in small ways through their everyday work.

Recommendation 7: Professional associations and journals should work in concert with funding agencies to create an infrastructure that takes advantage of technology to facilitate data sharing and knowledge accumulation in education research.

Advances in modern technology open avenues for the development of research infrastructure that facilitate the building of the knowledge base in education unimaginable just a few decades ago (National Research Council, 1985). In this context, we comment on the value of data repositories, registries of studies undertaken, bibliographic indexes of published studies, digitization of journal content, and open access models.

A host of existing data housing and data repository sites exist across many of the social and behavioral sciences, as well as in education research. The Inter-university Consortium for Political and Social Research (http://www.icpsr.umich.edu/org/index.html), for example, maintains and provides access to a vast archive of social science data, including education-related data, for research and instruction, and offers training in quantitative methods to facilitate effective data use. It was established in 1962, includes over 500 member colleges and universities, and encourages all social scientists to contribute to its data resources. The archive includes subparts, such as the National Archive of Criminal Justice Data, the Health and Medical Archive, and the International Archive of Education Data. The Henry A. Murray Research Center is a data archive dedicated to the study of lives over time. It is unique in that it holds many longitudinal studies and includes not only quantitative data, but also qualitative materials, such as case histories, open-ended interviews, and audio and video clips.

Data repositories can be powerful tools in the pursuit of scientific understanding in education. For example, they can be used to facilitate an accumulated knowledge base by encouraging the continued development of measures of key concepts in education research. In the context of dominant theories, these concepts and variables can be validated and revisited as investigators engage in new investigations over time, greatly facilitating integration across studies. In our view, attention is needed on how to encourage greater use of existing repositories as well as the possibility of developing new ones for facilitating data sharing and knowledge accumulation in education research.

Developing a single bibliographic index of education research studies—similar to the Educational Research Information Center (ERIC)—is another essential component of a technology-enabled infrastructure for education research. A fully elaborated resource not only should provide access to the full text of research documents and efficient and powerful searching tools for information retrieval, but also should be buttressed by a comprehensive indexing system that includes standardized definitions of key terms in an electronic thesaurus and clear standards for required descriptors of articles.

The process of developing such an indexing system requires specialized expertise and would be a multiyear undertaking. A multiyear effort spearheaded by the National Library of Medicine to develop a system for the biomedical sciences links to the keywords of major medical journals (Rothstein, 2003).

It is neither possible nor desirable to mandate single definitions of concepts for all of education research. Indeed, many changes in terminology are made in light of improved understanding of an issue. Overly restrictive standardization can straightjacket researchers and, ironically, stunt efforts to advance knowledge accumulation. Yet, it would be valuable to keep up-to-date definitions of major constructs in education through partnerships of associations like the AERA and federal agencies like the Institute of Education Studies (IES) that track, for example, a set of basic terms used in their journals and databases. Such efforts should recognize the importance of, and take into account, the testing of ideas and revision of measures and definitions over time and across different contexts. For example, definitions of measures could include relevant clarifications and differentiations that might arise when considering different student populations. When feasible, there should be links to appropriate data repositories. Ongoing discussions to promote such standards for methodological terms in particular within the International Campbell Collaboration[3] can provide helpful guidance. In implementing this recommendation, we also see the potential for an international effort that can bring together existing expertise, as well as for promoting policies that index terms across international contexts (e.g., relating the terms "elementary school" and "primary school").

---

[3]The international Campbell Collaboration is a nonprofit organization that aims to help people make well-informed decisions about the effects of interventions in the social, behavioral and educational arenas. Its objectives are to prepare, maintain and disseminate systematic reviews of studies of interventions (see www.campbellcollaboration.org).

Another mechanism to pursue as a long-term goal for facilitating knowledge accumulation is the establishment of a register of all education studies undertaken. Such a register would be different from a bibliographic database of all published studies (such as ERIC). One rationale for this kind of resource stems from the problem of publication bias. Publication bias, sometimes called the "file drawer problem," is the tendency for researchers to publish results that have positive results or effects and not to publish findings that have null, negative, or not statistically significant results (Iyengar and Greenhouse, 1988). Thus, efforts to synthesize existing work on a particular topic—including meta-analysis and the reviews currently being conducted by the What Works Clearinghouse—are at risk of being biased because of the systematic loss of statistically insignificant or negative study results or of being incomplete because studies are not available in published journals. In either case, systematic reviewing is unnecessarily laborious and expensive because hand searching and other ways of sifting through the "fugitive" literature are required. Another rationale for creating a single resource for researchers and consumers of research that contains information about ongoing work is that it could be a valuable tool for facilitating communication and collaboration among investigators working on similar issues and problems and for expanding access to relevant research among consumers of research.

Creating such a register of all studies undertaken is an ambitious undertaking. It would require navigating some thorny intellectual territory regarding what should be included in such a register: the vast quantity and divergent nature of the kinds of inquiries that might reasonably be considered education research will make the development of clear standards and protocols a difficult and probably contentious task. Clinicaltrials.gov, a federal effort to register trials of serious and life-threatening diseases, is an excellent model for one kind of study. A proposed effort to expand this register to include all initiated clinical trials in the near future offers initial lessons from which the education research communities could learn and begin their own dialogue about how to approach a similar undertaking.

Journals, too, can use technology to support similar aims at relatively low cost. Nearly 80 percent of scholarly journals are now available on-line (Willinsky, 2003). Indeed, the question is not if journals should be digitized but when, how, and for what purpose. Creating databases that house every article published by journals is technically feasible, and it offers a number of ways to promote quality and coherence in education research. For example, it enables the compilation of collections of related work to

---

BOX 3-2
The Value of Digital Journal Content

Gary Natriello, executive editor of the *Teachers College Record* (a peer-reviewed journal of Columbia University), has led an effort to digitize the journal's content and leverage the opportunities afforded by digitization for packaging material and opening channels for communication in ways that facilitate the building of a knowledge base over time. He described the innovative uses of *TCR* content enabled by the creation of *TC Record On-line* (www.tcrecord.org).

Natriello described digitization as providing the journal choices about how to bundle material in articles, series, or compilations. It also enables different formats and lengths, and innovative ways to represent articles. He said that it also offers the opportunity for two-way interaction. For example, the *TC Record On-line* publishes community discussion, in which they invite people to comment on articles and on themes and content and place that commentary on their home page.

In addition, the editorial team has edited collections of works, linked related materials across decades or longer, tracked the progress of a series of articles that developed over time, followed

---

illustrate the progression of a line of inquiry over time. Authors' names can be searched to identify potential reviewers by quickly allowing editors to view their publication records on the topic of a pending manuscript. Indeed, the power of digitized content is that it is flexible—innovative ideas for packaging and relating studies can be tried and studied at relatively low cost. Opening access through the Internet has important potential benefits to consider in the context of building the knowledge base: it can promote scholarly communication by allowing on-line dialogues on topics of interest, including critiques and reviews of published articles. See Box 3-2 for an example of how one education research journal has done so.

Finally, allowing consumers free or low-cost access to journals on-line in education can serve a very important function in helping to engage multiple audiences and extending the reach of these publications. Open access is a movement in publishing that innovatively seeks ways to provide access to users of content at no charge. Some journals, such as the AERA publica-

an author through his or her career, and "seized" teachable moments. Natriello also described plans for the next generation of the journal, in which they will convene groups of scholars around particular content areas, facilitate the group's interaction, and summarize and make available the results of that interaction to simulate an on-line consensus conference.

Another strategy *TC Record On-line* has attempted in order to facilitate greater knowledge accumulation is making data sets available on-line. Natriello told the group that the journal has offered to do that for authors for nearly five years, and no one has done so to date. The *TC Record On-line* team believes that their strategy for encouraging submission of data needs to change, so that they illustrate the process and power of this option by posting examples, paying people to do so, and exploring the use of other such incentives.

Workshop:	The Role of Journals in Developing the Education Research Knowledge Base
	November 11, 2003
	Transcript available at: http://www7.nationalacademies.org/core/
Key Speaker:	Gary Natriello, Teachers College, Columbia University

tion *Educational Researcher*, are free immediately and available around the world. Another example is the delayed open access provided by *Teachers College Record* and the *New England Journal of Medicine*, which open access six months after initial print publication. Lessons are beginning to emerge from the early experiences of several major journals that have experimented with this idea, and momentum is building to expand access to scientific findings in peer-reviewed journals. Indeed, the National Institutes of Health (NIH) recently invited comment on a proposed new requirement for NIH-funded researchers to provide articles accepted for publication to the agency so it can make them freely available six months after publication (see http://grants1.nih.gov/grants/guide/notice-files/NOT-OD-04-064.html). A major issue with opening access this way has to do with the financial losses that are likely to accrue to publishers. Some people have suggested that the losses stemming from declines in paid subscriptions be offset by generating revenue from authors as a condition of publication. An example of an on-

---

BOX 3-3
Using Technology and Expanding Access to Facilitate
Research Communication

John Willinsky described an effort called the Public Knowledge Project (http://www.pkp.ubc.ca/) that he has spearheaded to expand access to research through free (open access) online tools. He argued forcefully that a crucial dimension of the quality of research knowledge has to do with its circulation. Claims of research quality, he posited, are reduced by anything that unduly restricts the circulation of research, and this is becoming more a salient issue since access is declining in many institutions due to the high cost of journals.

Willinsky provided a demonstration of the journal management and publishing system that he has developed through the Public Knowledge Project. The Open Journal Systems was designed on three principles: it is free, it reduces the amount of work that is normally involved in editing by automating many of the processes, and it improves the scholarly and public quality of the research published. The premise is that access to tools that reduce publishing costs would provide an incentive to journals to make more of their work open to readers. The system is free to download and installs on any server. Editors and authors only need to do word processing and use fill-in web forms to use it. Open Journal Systems helps to manage the review process by allowing authors to upload their work, including supplementary files and data sets; by enabling reviewers to access these items and provide review comments all on an online basis; and by allowing editors to do their editing where they wish: in airport kiosks or lounges—anywhere there is a web

---

line open access content management tool is described in Box 3-3 and shows how such tools can benefit researchers and consumers alike.

Developing and fully exploiting each of these mechanisms will require care in ensuring that such infrastructure development and standardization be approached in a way that continues to encourage critique, questioning, exploration, and reconceptualizations. Actions that lead to constraining standardization will stifle innovation and crowd out talent. In our view, the field would benefit from the kind of careful foundational development called for in these recommendations by enabling advances across fields, investigators, and studies.

browser. Willinsky pointed out that this feature allows international teams of editors to begin to participate in journal publishing, which has historically been difficult due to the need for centralization.

As he described it, one innovation of this system is that it provides journals using it with a research support tool to accompany each published article. The research support tool provides readers an "information context" that supports the public's ability to interpret and use relevant research-based information. He argued that the public has an interest in research when it is directly concerned with what they are doing. They have the motivation, he argued, but not sufficient context to interpret the research. Thus, the research support tool identifies, for example, that an article is peer reviewed; it also allows readers to readily locate related studies in the Educational Research Information Center database, to help them see that "no study is an island unto itself." The system also includes links to other relevant resources associated with the author's keywords, such as FirstGov (www.first.gov), a website that taps into U.S. government websites as well as the websites of all states. Willinsky informed the group that the tool is currently being tested with policy makers in Ottawa as a way of assessing how open access publishing can increase research's impact on policy.

Workshop:	The Role of Journals in Developing the Education Research Knowledge Base
	November 11, 2003
	Transcript available at: http://www7.nationalacademies.org/core/
Key Speaker:	John Willinsky, University of British Columbia

Building infrastructure takes time. No single journal, scientific association, or federal agency could build these tools alone. We call on the major institutional players in education research—the AERA and the IES (especially ERIC)—to provide the leadership and resources to explore and encourage these kinds of efforts and to set priorities for implementation in light of resource availability over time. We also see a role for the major philanthropic foundations that support education research to make these ideas a reality. It will take the combined efforts of these institutions to marshal the resources that will be required.

Recommendation 8: Education research journals should develop and implement policies requiring structured abstracts.

Abstracts are short summaries that accompany full-length articles, and they can also appear independently to summarize presentations given at meetings. Abstracts serve a number of purposes. One of the most important is to allow other researchers and consumers of research to easily obtain information about the key elements of published studies. Such information enables researchers working on an issue to find related work, enhancing the likelihood that relevant bodies of work can be identified and interpreted to promote an accumulated knowledge base over time. In a similar way, structured abstracts would also promote better utilization of education research.

A recent article published in *Educational Researcher* (Mosteller, Nave, and Miech, 2004) made this case convincingly, offering a prototype structure for consideration by the education research communities and associated journals. Proposed elements of structured abstracts include background/context; purpose/objective/research question/focus of study; setting; populations/participants/research subjects; intervention/program/practice; research design; data collection and analysis; findings and results; and conclusions and recommendations (p. 32). It is important to recognize that following a sequential format in structured abstracts may not be appropriate for all kinds of education research (e.g., the goal of some anthropological work is to generate a question, rather than to address a question or test a hypothesis). Including a common set of information in these abstracts, such as those described in the Mosteller et al. article, is the key.

Beyond the generalized benefits the field could realize from structured abstracts, the early experience of several recent efforts to synthesize high-quality education research on topics of importance to policy and practice has provided an additional rationale and sense of urgency for implementing a policy of structured abstracts in education research journals. The International Campbell Collaboration and the federally funded What Works Clearinghouse are both developing systematic, rigorous, and transparent processes for summarizing research findings and ways to communicate those summaries to educators who can most benefit from them. Many of the technical challenges associated with creating these resources stem from problems in accessing and summarizing articles from scholarly journals to synthesize social science research. Structured abstracts would help alleviate these problems.

Workshop speakers with expertise in systematic reviewing argued that to date, the process of systematic reviewing has been hampered by the very poor quality of abstracts and, in some cases, very misleading titles of articles. This problem is compounded by the fact that electronic abstracts are often less useful than the actual hard copies: for example, the Educational Resources Information Center—the primary database for education research articles—reduces authors' abstracts, often resulting in their missing some of the crucial information needed for systematic review information retrieval and analysis (Rothstein, 2003; Sebba, 2003).

The way in which current abstracts fail most often is in providing an adequate description of the characteristics of the sample (Sebba, 2003). For example, a study may involve only ethnic minorities or elementary school students, but the abstract does not specify the age group or the race/ethnicity of the sample used in the study. A requirement for structured abstracts, coupled with greater attention to the quality of abstracts by editors and publishers, would go a long way in producing abstracts that are readable, well organized, brief, and self-contained and that facilitate the systematic review process (Hartley, 1997). Developing standards for structured abstracts should be done internationally, so that terms that vary across borders can be defined and referenced.

In sum, abstracts are critical to the information retrieval process for developing systematic reviews and meta-analyses to sift through and to identify the universe of relevant research. When these abstracts fail to contain basic information about the study objective, sample strategy, research design, and other key features of research, any searching process becomes intensely laborious, slowing the work considerably. Furthermore, missing relevant articles has the potential to bias the summary results by skewing the sample of studies selected for review. Implementation of a standardized format for abstracts in journals is a relatively easy yet powerful change for journals to make to facilitate such reviews (Ad Hoc Working Group for Critical Appraisal of the Medical Literature, 1987).

CONCLUSION

Most codes of ethics that specify professional norms and expectations for social scientists include standards for ways in which individual investigators are responsible for contributing to their field as a whole. Many of these standards relate directly to the kinds of efforts we recommend be taken to build a knowledge base in education research that accumulates over time through better and more frequent communications and data sharing. Therefore, most of what we call for is not new: rather, they are policies and practices that have been neglected; they deserve renewed attention.

4

Enhancing Professional Development

The need for a diverse pool of well-trained education researchers to generate high-quality scholarship and to lend their expertise to deliberations about educational practice and policy is great. As in any other professional endeavor, attention to ways in which education researchers are trained and provided with opportunities for continued growth over the course of their careers is essential. We focus on a few such opportunities: doctoral training in schools of education, and peer review panels for judging both education research proposals (submitted to federal agencies), and products (articles submitted to journals for publication).

NATURE OF THE FIELD

Approaching the crucial topic of how to frame and develop high-quality professional development for education researchers requires an appreciation of the diversity of the field and the kinds of students who pursue advanced training. Education researchers come from virtually every discipline and from many interdisciplinary specialties, reside in a great variety of institutions—schools of education, university arts and science departments, and now even policy schools and schools of management, think tanks, and school systems—and focus on an enormous array of research topics.

Furthermore, novices in education research usually enter the field relatively late—beginning academic study of education research only when they become doctoral students. Many have previously studied to be teachers and gained considerable teaching experience, but they have no prior training or experience conducting research. For some, their undergraduate and master's programs were in content areas (e.g., mathematics, English, history, biology). For others, undergraduate and master's work may have been in one of the social science disciplines. Still others completed master's degrees oriented toward the skills of practice in teaching, counseling, or school administration, with limited attention to the conduct of research.

Available data suggest that there are 1,000 Ph.D.-level degrees awarded in education research each year (Levine, 2003). Compared with the production of Ph.D.s in social and behavioral sciences fields, this number is quite large. However, the real issue may not be one of quantity, but one of quality: Are current and prospective education researchers capable of tackling the complex questions that policy makers and practitioners want answers to? And more to the point: Are existing training and professional development activities producing a capable cadre of investigators?

MECHANISMS FOR ENHANCING PROFESSIONAL DEVELOPMENT

These are tough questions without simple answers. Our work only scratched the surface but nonetheless resulted in several promising suggestions for positive change. In this chapter, we focus on three leverage points: schools of education, peer review processes in federal agencies, and the policies and practices of publishers, especially peer-reviewed journals.

Schools of Education

Although education researchers pursue advanced training in a variety of institutions and university departments, we chose to focus our recommendations on the role of doctoral programs in schools of education because of their central role in preparing the next generation of leaders in education research. Our focus is on those schools of education that prepare researchers (many do not, their sole purpose being to provide advanced training for educators and administrators), recognizing that even among this smaller set of schools, there are substantial differences in the origins and nature of schools of education across the country.

As we have said, the kinds of students who choose to enroll in doctoral programs in schools of education vary dramatically. Because there are so many pathways for pursuing academic preparation in education research, recruitment strategies at doctoral programs in schools of education must reach out to students with a range of academic and professional backgrounds to tap the available pool of talent. This necessity means that groups of future education researchers who embark on doctoral training in schools of education have a wide range of skills, experiences, and world views to bring to their work—a real asset to a field as complex as education research. Schools of education can and should recruit students from a range of social, racial, and economic backgrounds as well (Hancock, 2003). This diversity can strengthen the quality of research in the field by effectively tapping a broad pool of talent and by promoting research that is relevant to a range of education issues and student populations.

When a diverse group of students comes together in a doctoral program, however, they do not share previous experiences, a common language, or norms regarding the value and conduct of education research. Doctoral programs in schools of education play a particularly crucial role in helping to define and instill common principles and habits of mind that will grow with them as they pursue their careers in education research and contribute to the knowledge base (Labaree, 2003).

Still, doctoral training of education researchers and the challenges associated with it are at their core very similar across social and behavioral science disciplines, as well as professional fields like social work, business, and nursing. For example, scholars and educators in social, behavioral, and economic sciences are increasingly aware of the need for advanced skills and methodological tools to address the vexing problems facing society, not unlike education research. In these disciplines there is also appreciation that training requires enhanced, interdisciplinary integration across related fields, again, quite similar to issues facing education research trainers. There are also similarities between education research training and training in other professional fields. Social work, for example, is much more akin to education in aspiring to build conceptual and methodological scientific skill, and many of the current concerns in the social work field about doctoral training have parallels to education research. Further, the ongoing tension in doctoral programs in social work between the objective of preparing high-quality researchers to go to top schools and the objective of training faculty with broad knowledge and excellent teaching skills, who can work in social work programs ranging from very large to very small, is present in doctoral programs housed in schools of education. Furthermore, while some doctoral programs in social work focus on clinical practice, more focus on research, and some are trying to make the transition to a research focus or create a balance between the two (Levine, 2003).

Mindful of these similarities and differences, we adopt the premise of the Carnegie Initiative on the Doctorate (see Box 4-1) as an organizing idea for our recommendations regarding doctoral programs for education researchers in schools of education. This initiative is supporting reforms in doctoral programs in a range of fields, including education, with the overarching goal of using doctoral training to develop a professional community with shared norms, language, and ways of knowing. Doctoral training can and should be a mechanism for instilling common habits of mind—not rote standardization, but a sense of purpose around which research and teaching can be framed.

Recommendation 9: Schools of education that train doctoral students for careers in education research should articulate the competencies their research graduates should know and be able to do and design their programs to enable students to develop them.

Schools of education did not begin life as research centers. Rather their origins lie in 19th century normal schools, which were designed to provide roughly one additional year of schooling to would-be teachers.[1] Subsequently, as normal schools evolved into teacher's colleges and as research universities added schools or departments of education, research was undertaken either as a basis for generating a curriculum or as outreach to local schools. As a result, research that is congruent with the principles of science is a very recent arrival in schools of education. Developing earlier in some fields—notably psychology—scientific research became generally important in schools of education only in the 1960s, when the marriage of education studies and social science disciplines—history, philosophy, anthropology, psychology, sociology, and economics—established the importance of rigorous methods (Lagemann, 2000).

Not surprisingly, given this situation, no two schools of education prepare researchers in exactly the same way. Some schools award Ed.D. degrees; others give Ph.D.s; others give both. (Indeed, it is not even clear what the differences between the two degrees are, as their purposes and require-

---

[1]There are substantial differences in origin among the schools of education across the country; normal schools are one common origin.

BOX 4-1
Carnegie Initiative on the Doctorate

Lee Shulman emphasized the idea that while doctoral training in education research is different in important ways from other fields, lessons can be learned from exploring the experiences of other institutions and departments. Echoing other speakers' remarks about the striking similarities between education research training issues and those in other fields, Shulman offered the example of recent discussions about doctoral training in mathematics, in which leading scholars identified as a core problem the development of an understanding of the boundaries between mathematics as a discipline and mathematics as a profession; education is similarly vexed. He also pointed to law schools—which, like education schools—draw a student body with a diverse set of educational backgrounds, yet have common courses and other similarities that cut across the first year of their doctoral programs, providing a common basis for their advanced training and professional lives—unlike education schools. He further suggested that in some ways, reform of doctoral education in education schools is far ahead of what it is in other sciences to which education research is often derisively compared.

Shulman described some of the efforts to foster the improvement of doctoral training that he has spearheaded in the Carnegie Initiative on the Doctorate (see http://www.carnegiefoundation.org/CID/). The initiative endeavors to enrich and invigorate doctoral education through a multi-year research program. Envisioned is the idea of preparing "stewards of the disciplines"—individuals who can generate new knowledge and defend against challenges and criti-

---

ments vary substantially across universities.) Some schools encourage research on teaching practice; others focus on policy research. Some schools require training in statistics; others do not. Some require experience collecting data in the field; others do not. Some require participation in supervised research and preparation of a scholarly publication prior to graduation; others do not. As currently constituted, such doctoral programs do little to ensure that the preparation of education researchers meets at least a minimal standard of scholarly rigor.

The workshop on doctoral programs at education schools illustrated the importance of articulating a common core of education that can shape

cisms while conserving important ideas and findings from past work in their disciplines. Such individuals will be able to transform knowledge into "powerful pedagogies of engagement, understanding, and application" (Golde and Walker, 2002).

The initiative has been explicitly designed to promote cross-disciplinary and cross-departmental thinking and learning in the pursuit of improving doctoral training in the areas of English, chemistry, mathematics, history, neuroscience, and education. It has provided financial support for 50 partner departments at colleges and universities across the United States to conduct "design experiments" in which they examine the purposes and desired outcomes of their doctoral programs and consider what changes to their programs are needed to better achieve outcome goals, including fostering stewardship of the discipline. The initiative has also convened discipline-specific conferences where representatives from the partner departments can discuss and learn from one another's efforts. Several products will result from these efforts, including models of experimental doctoral programs, research and analysis of the sponsored efforts, and institutional and policy-level recommendations.

Workshop: A National Conversation About Doctoral
            Programs for Future Leaders in
            Education Research
            November 12, 2003
            Transcript available at: http://
            www7.nationalacademies.org/core/
Key Speaker: Lee Shulman, Carnegie Foundation for
            the Advancement of Teaching

the development of advanced research training. What are the core courses every education researcher ought to have to earn their doctorate? Without an articulation of what graduates need to know, there is no reference point from which to design course sequences. How should research apprenticeships and experiences in these core competencies be structured? It depends on what it is you want students to gain from those experiences. Lacking direction on the goals, mapping out roles and responsibilities across organizational lines is problematic.

Specifying the competencies that every graduate of doctoral programs in schools of education—that is, the future leaders in education research—

should have is critical. Not only would such an exercise provide an essential lens for developing and implementing training programs, it would result in an articulation of a minimum breadth of skills and experiences all education researchers should have. Such an articulation is important because the field is so diverse and because its participants need to recognize the role, value, and points of convergence across a range of theoretical ideas, epistemologies, and methods.

It is likely that many schools of education would need to articulate these competencies at the level of the program—for example, an educational psychology program that trains education researchers would be likely to articulate some different goals for its doctoral students than a similar program in a curriculum and instruction department. However, there also may be some goals that schools have for all of their students, as is the case in the School of Education at the University of Colorado, Boulder (see Box 4-2). In either case, schools or programs would articulate what skills and experiences they want students to have when they complete their doctoral training and then design the curriculum, apprenticeships, mentoring, and research experiences needed to develop that base of substantive and methodological knowledge.

At the workshop we learned about some promising initiatives by administrators and schools across the country working to find creative ways of approaching this issue. With careful planning, study, and leadership, the potential is great.

Recommendation 10: Schools of education that train doctoral students for careers in education research should design their programs to enable research students to develop deep substantive and methodological knowledge and skill in a specialized area.

In addition to facilitating a breadth of knowledge in education research among doctoral candidates, schools of education should also provide opportunities for students to develop a depth of expertise in selected subfields of education research. As students progress through their doctoral training, their course work and research experiences should hone their skills and understanding in the theoretical ideas, methodological tools, and existing research in the subfield they intend to pursue over the course of their careers.

It is in the development of deep expertise in subfields of education research that collaborations with disciplinary departments and other orga-

BOX 4-2
Designing a Core Curriculum for Education Research Doctoral Candidates

Margaret Eisenhart described a recent effort at the University of Colorado that she led to develop a core curriculum for their doctoral students studying to become education researchers. She and her colleagues embarked on this work after the faculty agreed that the existing doctoral program was not adequately preparing students to conduct high-quality education research. To inform development of a new program, Eisenhart and a faculty committee examined basic data on leading education schools, including the content and number of required courses. They found that beyond one or two required methods courses, there was very little that was common across or even within most schools. The committee found this lack of a common set of courses especially problematic given the nature of their graduate students: many are former teachers, and many lack the kind of undergraduate preparation that is typical in discipline-based research trajectories. Furthermore, students without research training also sometimes approached their graduate work with a deep skepticism of research and its utility for helping to solve problems in education.

Eisenhart and her colleagues designed a set of core courses for their doctoral students in light of these facts: they explicitly sought to develop a common language, to convey and discuss a shared set of issues and arguments in the field, and to instill common norms and standards for the conduct of research. Eisenhart described several challenges in designing their curriculum, including the difficulty of balancing breadth and depth: the faculty believed that students should have a general understanding of the field of education and education research, but also develop deep expertise in a substantive area and a set of research methodologies.

The process that Eisenhart led at Boulder was supported by students but complicated by some faculty resistance. She told the group that many faculty were wary of change for several reasons, including tradition, the burden of developing and teaching new courses, and fears that those specialty areas represented in the core curriculum would have disproportional influence and control over all students' thinking in the early stages of their training.

The faculty involved in this effort are also focused on ensuring that all students, regardless of their backgrounds prior to beginning

Continued

doctoral work, have access to both teaching and research experiences as part of the program. It is relatively easy to assign former teachers to teaching assistantships, and it is easy for students with research training to be included in faculty research grants. It is less easy but crucial to the success of their program to cross those lines, according to Eisenhart.

The faculty committee that spearheaded the new program worked hard to overcome these obstacles.[a] One strategy was to assemble a broadly representative planning committee and to offer multiple opportunities for faculty updates and input on the committee's work. The planning committee also received strong backing from the dean and the help of the Carnegie Initiative on the Doctorate, a national effort to consider reforms in graduate research training across a range of disciplines (see Box 4-1).

After a year and half of work, Eisenhart and her colleagues received approval from the full faculty for a three-year doctoral curriculum, anchored by a required core for first-year students. The new curriculum includes the following courses:

Year 1 (all first-year students will take these courses together as a cohort)
- Six required common courses, three per semester, including:
  — Two "big ideas" courses (semester 1 will focus on research about teaching and learning in classrooms; semester 2 will focus on how research informs educational policies)
  — Two qualitative methods courses (one each semester)
  — Two quantitative methods courses (one each semester)
  — Each semester, two cross-cutting topics will be taken up simultaneously in the three courses as a means of integrating the core course material

nizational entities in a university can pay off, particularly for in-depth methodological training. Indeed, education faculty expertise and school of education offerings are not likely to cover all specializations adequately. Opportunities to take courses or to work with faculty outside the school of education can facilitate the honing of specialized expertise by expanding access to a wider range of subfields and specialty areas (Raudenbush, 2003).

We readily acknowledge that collaborations across units of complex organizations like universities are difficult to establish and sustain. Difficult or not, we conclude that to promote the highest caliber of education re-

- Two informal seminars in student's chosen specialty area (one each semester)

Year 2
- Focused course work in specialty area (content and method)
- Multicultural seminar (a required course retained from the old program requirements)

Year 3
- Advanced course work in specialty area and preparation of dissertation proposal

Workshop:	A National Conversation About Doctoral Programs for Future Leaders in Education Research November 12, 2003 Transcript available at: http://www7.nationalacademies.org/core/
Key Speaker:	Margaret Eisenhart, University of Colorado

---

[a]Some elements of the doctoral program described here are still in planning stages, and implementation was not scheduled to begin until fall 2004. Thus, it remains to be seen how well the changes will be implemented, what additional resistance will occur, and the extent to which the new program actually furthers the faculty's goals.

searchers, they are essential, and they have been brokered successfully in the past: for example, progress in statistical modeling and causal inference can be attributed at least in part to scholars trained in statistics with joint appointments in education and statistics departments (Raudenbush, 2003).

Why are such collaborations necessary? Training education researchers exclusively in disciplinary departments robs the profession of a common core and can detach investigators from the central issues in education they espouse to study. Training education researchers exclusively in schools of education shuts students off from the social and behavioral sciences and related departments, stunting opportunities for in-depth explorations and depriving the future leaders in the field of relevant disciplinary models and methods. The way to address this "essential tension" (Shulman, 2003) is to make the boundaries between the two organizational units highly permeable: that is, to actively encourage research collaborations among the faculty and students in each around common areas of inquiry (Tobin, 2003). Formal arrangements like dual degrees, requirements for minors, or joint appointments are possible; informal links among individual faculty members are essential. Typical incentive structures at some universities will have to change in order to support the forging of such links.

Thus, the university itself will need to enable these connections by actively supporting and encouraging them. New syllabi for courses need to get approval from the university curriculum committee. Scheduling changes to accommodate greater interactions within cohorts of students and across university departments will be required. Beyond these more rudimentary challenges are long-standing funding discrepancies and shortfalls. Universities can and should actively support such collaborations financially.

Recommendation 11: Schools of education that train doctoral students for careers in education research should provide all students with a variety of meaningful research experiences.

It is hard to overstate the importance of providing regular and increasingly sophisticated opportunities to design and conduct education research in doctoral programs. Research experience is absolutely essential—without applying the concepts covered in course work, they are mere abstractions, and research skill is difficult to develop. Furthermore, opportunities for publication and other professional networking experiences are limited without contributing to ongoing research projects.

In addressing how such experiences might be structured, the traditional vehicle of the dissertation needs reconsideration. One lone project conducted alone at the end of a program squelches opportunities to learn from multiple experiences and flies in the face of the idea of teams of researchers working together on common problems. A better model might be for doctoral students to develop a portfolio of research products (Cohen, 2003; Shulman, 2003; Whitehurst, 2003). Staging a series of research experiences would also provide opportunities to publish research findings in peer-reviewed journals, and to present at conferences.

Ensuring meaningful research experiences for doctoral students requires that they engage in research under the guidance of multiple faculty members who themselves are active in the field. Indeed, such mentorships are a key feature of the professional development of junior scholars in many scientific disciplines. Seasoned investigators active in education research can help facilitate the kinds of access, opportunities, and networking so critical to establishing junior researchers as contributors to their profession.

In doctoral programs for education researchers, traditional one-on-one mentoring might be augmented or even replaced by participation in interdisciplinary networks that connect faculty and students in schools of education with their peers in other departments. This kind of work may be especially important for doctoral students who have no prior research experience—former teachers, for example—to help orient them into the culture of research and to provide a setting in which their expertise can be tapped systematically. The importance of collaborations with disciplinary departments is relevant for promoting meaningful research experiences as well, because they provide opportunities for students to develop their specializations and to interact with faculty members conducting research outside schools of education.

Finally, an important element in the research experiences of doctoral students pursuing careers in education research is that they engage in research-based interactions with schools or other educational settings. Such interactions are likely to pay off in a number of ways. Working in schools provides the real-world conceptual context for graduate research training—the understanding of major issues facing educators and administrators today. In the context of conducting research, working together with practitioners also serves the very practical end of developing researchers who know how to set up and implement research projects conducted on site: providing these opportunities could help address concerns we heard at our workshops that many education researchers do not know how to work with urban schools.

To seasoned administrators in schools of education, these recommendations may seem wholly unattainable in the face of available resources. It is absolutely true that high-quality doctoral training for researchers requires a good deal of time for both students and the faculty members supervising them and time, of course, means money. The ways in which schools of education are financed, however, vary, and similarities and differences in the financial underpinnings across institutions are not widely understood. An analysis of these issues would greatly facilitate institution- and policy-level action to strengthen doctoral training for education researchers.

One aspect of such an analysis would need to focus on student financial support and patterns of program completion. Strong research training typically requires full-time study. And full-time study typically requires financial support. However, National Center for Education Statistics data reveal that 50 percent of doctoral students in education receive no financial support. By contrast, in the humanities and the physical, life, and social sciences, just 21 percent of students receive no support. The federal government needs to provide funds to enable in-depth research training (Whitehurst, 2003) of the kind we call for here; programs funded by other organizations like private foundations will also likely be necessary.

The improvement of education research training is a core matter of professional responsibility for the field (Cohen, 2003). Marshalling the financial and intellectual resources for it is a crucial task.

Federal Agencies

Professional development in education research does not begin or end with doctoral programs in schools of education. In this section we highlight participation in peer review panels in federal agencies that fund education research as an effective mechanism to provide ongoing professional development of education researchers at all stages of their careers.

Although not typically viewed in this way federal agencies can contribute to the professional development of the field through their peer review processes. Participating in peer review has a powerful influence on shaping education research professionals and the quality of their future work. Several ways in which these peer review systems can be designed to promote the professional development of the field are described in detail in *Strengthening Peer Review in Federal Agencies That Support Education Research* (National Research Council, 2004b). Here, we reprise the role of peer review as a tool for enhancing the professional development of education researchers.

Recommendation 12: Peer review panels in federal agencies that fund education research should be composed to promote the participation of people from a range of scholarly perspectives and traditionally underrepresented groups and provide opportunities for professional development.

In Chapter 2 we argued that diversity in peer review panels promoted quality. Here, we focus on another way that actively recruiting panelists from diverse backgrounds to participate in the process can improve the process: by extending professional opportunity to a broader pool of researchers, building capacity in the field as a whole. Social characteristics affect the training researchers receive (because of the schools they attend, the topics and designs they are likely to pursue in school, and the jobs they anticipate for themselves) and in turn affect the experiences and expertise they develop (Harding, 1991; Howe, 2004). Thus, explicit attempts to engage traditionally underrepresented groups in the peer review process can improve access and opportunity, resulting in an overall stronger field and more relevant research.

Peer review can provide a rich context for further developing researchers into the culture of their profession and should be explicitly designed to promote the attainment of this objective. This function of peer review is often underutilized in the push to make funding decisions efficiently. Opportunities for engaging panel members in activities that further their professional development are facilitated when panels include broad representation of relevant experience and expertise, when panel members deliberate together, and when time permits differences of perspective and position to be aired and debated. Such opportunities for developing investigators— both experienced and inexperienced with respect to sitting on review panels—to the research ethos are facilitated when clear requests for proposals are available and when good feedback is provided to proposers. These conditions also create incentives for strong researchers to contribute their time and expertise to peer review: Why should they contribute if so little will come of their efforts and if they will gain so little from the experience?

Involving promising scholars in peer review at early stages of their careers can also target professional development opportunities for up-and-coming researchers who have solid credentials but less experience reviewing. The testaments of many workshop participants citing early experiences serving on National Institutes of Health (standing) panels as career-changing are indications of the potential of peer review to develop early career researchers. It is important, however, that promoting the participation of rising scholars in the context of peer review be balanced against the need to tap the best intellectual talent for review.

We need to be clear that by supporting peer review as a mechanism for developing researchers, the committee is not arguing for inculcating researchers to a culture based on cronyism and traditionalism. To prevent the isolation of perspectives and favoritism for well-established names and institutions from taking hold, checks on the system must be in place. That said, the very foundation of the research process rests on the development of a commitment to scientific norms and values, which can and should be reinforced in the context of peer review (National Research Council, 2002).

Publishers

The rationale to target the publication process as a means for professional development is exactly as it is for federal funding agencies: publishers of peer-reviewed education research have the opportunity and the responsibility to view and to develop their manuscript review procedures in ways that promote the professional development of those involved, particularly researchers who submit manuscripts for publication.

Recommendation 13: Publishers of peer-reviewed education research should design their editorial and manuscript review systems to promote the professional development of education researchers who participate in that process.

If done well, reviews of manuscripts are conducted by established researchers in the field with a range of perspectives and types of expertise, and their judgments can be helpful in shaping the future work of the prospective author. Thus, the ideas we put forth about diversity with respect to proposal review in federal agencies apply equally to manuscript review: encouraging highly qualified researchers from a range of backgrounds, perspectives, and career levels can promote a vibrant stock of published articles and facilitate growth and development among a wider range of scholars. The main difference is that professional development opportunities are likely to center largely on those submitting manuscripts, because reviewers and editors do not typically collaborate closely on reviews of manuscripts and therefore have less opportunity for the interaction that is the core of professional development.

All of the journals represented at the committee's workshop provided feedback one way or another to authors of submitted manuscripts (usually in the form of blinded copies of the original reviews)—and many of them expressed their view that the review process served an important educative function in addition to its role as a screening device. Several of the editors at the workshop cited this goal as an explicit one in their work, one calling the work "developmental" editing (Emihovich, 2003). Others pointed to the inclusion of more junior scholars as reviewers as evidence of their commitment to this idea (Coughlin, 2003). Yet the ability to provide this kind of feedback, as many editors and others involved in publishing journals attested, is limited by the logistical burdens that many social science and education journals place on their editors (McKeown, 2003). See Box 3-3 for a description of a tool designed to ease this burden and free up time for editors to engage in the professional development of scholars in their respected fields.

Our recommendation to publishers has a number of corollaries. One is that we think most manuscripts deserve some kind of review. While the participants at the workshop all rejected some small fraction of submissions without formal review, even in those cases, many of the editors revealed that they would write personal rationales and critiques to encourage high-quality future submissions. While enacting this recommendation will require more time on the part of editors, if the logistical burdens of publishing are eased, editors will have more time to engage in important substantive interactions that can slowly build capacity. The second corollary is that journals should consider revise and resubmit policies to enable the results of the reviews to promote improved future manuscripts.

CONCLUSION

Our recommendations for the professional development of education researchers are necessarily limited in scope. Doctoral programs in schools of education, as well as participation in peer review within federal funding agencies and journals, play important roles in reinforcing the norms and standards of the community. However, in our view the professional development of education researchers is a critical area for sustained analysis. Future work might seek to look at how to recruit and prepare education researchers earlier in their careers—in undergraduate programs, for example, and to conceptualize the professional development as a continuum of experiences over the course of a variety of career trajectories.

5

Summary and Conclusion

In this final chapter, we present all of the committee's recommendations and suggest directions for future work in advancing scientific research in education.

RECOMMENDATIONS

Recommendation 1. In federal agencies that support education research, the criteria by which peer reviewers rate proposals should be clearly delineated, and the meaning of different score levels on each scale should be defined and illustrated. Reviewers should be trained in the use of these scales.

Recommendation 2. Federal agencies that support education research should ensure that as a group, each peer review panel should have the research experience and expertise to judge the theoretical and technical merits of the proposals it reviews. In addition, peer review panels should be composed so as to minimize conflicts of interest and balance biases and promote the participation of people from a range of scholarly perspectives and traditionally underrepresented groups.

Recommendation 3. In research conducted in educational settings, investigators must not only select rigorous methods appropriate to the questions posed but also implement them in ways that meet the highest standards of evidence for those questions and methods.

Recommendation 4. Federal agencies should ensure appropriate resources are available for education researchers conducting large-scale investigations in educational settings to build partnerships with practitioners and policy makers.

Recommendation 5. Professional associations involved in education research should develop explicit ethical standards for data sharing.

Recommendation 6. Education research journals should require authors to make relevant data available to other researchers as a condition of publication and to ensure that applicable ethical standards are upheld.

Recommendation 7. Professional associations and education research journals should work in concert with funding agencies to create an infrastructure that takes advantage of technology to facilitate data sharing and knowledge accumulation in education research.

Recommendation 8. Education research journals should develop and implement policies requiring structured abstracts.

Recommendation 9. Schools of education that train doctoral students for careers in education research should articulate the competencies their research graduates should know and be able to do and design their programs to enable students to develop them.

Recommendation 10. Schools of education that train doctoral students for careers in education research should design their programs to enable research students to develop deep substantive and methodological knowledge and skill in a specialized area.

Recommendation 11. Schools of education that train doctoral students for careers in education research should provide all students with a variety of meaningful research experiences.

Recommendation 12. Peer review panels in federal agencies that fund education research should be composed to promote the participation of people from a range of scholarly perspectives and traditionally underrepresented groups and provide opportunities for professional development.

Recommendation 13. Publishers of peer-reviewed education research should design their editorial and manuscript review systems to promote the professional development of education researchers who participate in that process.

RECOMMENDATIONS BY TARGET AUDIENCE

The target audiences for this report are education researchers and the institutions that support them. Most of the recommendations we make will require effort on the part of individual researchers as well as multiple organizations. Table 5-1 organizes the recommendations according to the organizational entity that will need to lead its implementation; each has a role in pursuing the three strategic objectives of promoting quality, building the knowledge base, and enhancing the professional development of researchers. The three central organizations targeted are federal research agencies that support education research, professional associations and publishers of education research, and schools of education and universities.

The first column of the table reflects the lead role we envision for federal agencies in implementing recommendations related to promoting quality—they design the peer review systems that play a critical role in judging the quality of proposed work; they are a centralized source of financial support that can and should invest in critical infrastructure needs; and they can facilitate the development of partnerships between researchers and educators by supporting them both substantively and financially when funding large-scale research projects. Other organizations that rely on peer review—for example, philanthropic foundations in their grant-making processes and professional associations in the development of their annual meeting agendas—can and should play a similar role in designing their peer review systems to promote high quality scholarship. We also highlight the role that peer review systems in federal agencies can play in ongoing professional development of a diverse set of education researchers as another unsung yet powerful vehicle for enhancing the professional development of the field.

The middle column highlights the central role of professional associations like the American Educational Research Association (AERA) in developing a knowledge base of education research that accumulates over time.

TABLE 5-1 Recommendations by Lead Target Audience

Federal Research Agencies	Professional Associations and Publishers	Schools of Education and Universities
• Define and enforce peer review quality criteria (1) • Ensure peer reviewer expertise and diversity (2) • Fund research partnerships (4) • Create infrastructure to facilitate data sharing and knowledge accumulation (7) • Maximize participation of peer reviewers from different scholarly perspectives and traditionally underrepresented groups (12)	• Develop explicit standards for data sharing (5) • Require authors of journal articles to make data available to other researchers (6) • Create infrastructure to facilitate data sharing and knowledge accumulation (7) • Develop standards for structured abstracts (8) • Develop manuscript review systems that support professional development (13)	• Articulate and enable development of competencies for students pursuing education research careers (9) • Ensure students pursuing education research careers develop deep substantive and methodological knowledge (10) • Provide students pursuing education research careers with variety of meaningful research experiences (11)

NOTES: Recommendation numbers appear in parentheses, and language has been shortened to fit the table. Recommendation 3 is not included because it is aimed at individual investigators rather than an institutional audience. Recommendation 7 appears twice because it calls for a partnership between federal agencies and professional associations to lead its implementation.

AERA and related membership associations are a natural place to spearhead further infrastructure development by, for example, providing a forum for groups of individual investigators to explore avenues for implementation of these recommendations. In partnership with federal funding agencies, these associations should take a leadership role in developing an infrastructure that supports the development, maintenance, and use of databases, data repositories, and registries. Through policy changes, associations should actively encourage the sharing of data by incorporating an explicit standard into their ethical guidelines that pertain to investigators' responsibility to the field. They should also tie the publication requirements of association journals to that standard by mandating authors to make relevant data available to competent researchers and by creating manuscript review processes that facilitate professional growth among education researchers.

Finally, in the last column we target schools of education and university leaders to reinforce their central role in promoting the development of a highly competent field of education researchers. Schools of education are most commonly known for training educators and administrators, but the role of those schools that offer doctoral programs in education research deserves far greater attention both within individual departments and at the highest ranks of university leadership. These programs are a key leverage point for developing a talented pool of education researchers capable of tackling the next generation of challenging research questions. Schools of education and universities can also play an important role in promoting quality by infusing high standards of rigor into the pursuit of both teaching (e.g., through the development of coursework, research experiences, and experiences working with schools and districts for students) and research (e.g., through hiring, tenure, promotion, and other mechanisms that reward faculty for scholarly contributions). They might also play a role in developing effective peer reviewers in their training programs, in promoting the participation of future teachers and administrators in education research through their Ed.D. or related degree programs.

Additionally, while not called out in our recommendations specifically, schools of education play a central role in training future education researchers to value, and to be competent in conducting, research that integrates, replicates, or summarizes existing data or publications. The recognition of the value of such work in developing a knowledge base should be reflected in the incentives that are built into the tenure and promotion policies of the universities and schools as well.

No one institution could or should implement these recommendations alone. Rather, to promote improvements in education research capacity and infrastructure as broadly defined by the committee, their implementation will require leadership and resources from the many organizations and individual investigators that constitute the diverse and diffuse field of education research. For example, we call on the major professional associations to develop standards for data sharing in Recommendation 5. The extent to which these standards are met and followed among education researchers, however, depends greatly on explicit support for data sharing by federal agencies and universities, through, for example, providing financial support to investigators to prepare their data for reuse and acknowledging the development of protocols for data sharing as a meaningful, scholarly contribution, respectively. Also, although we did not focus on the role of foundations in our work, they are certainly prime candidates for partnering in the implementation of the infrastructure-building recommendations in particular, and their potential contributions should be considered and encouraged.

The committee's recommendations are geared to the objective they most directly serve in the advancement of scientific education research: promoting quality, developing an accumulated knowledge base, and enhancing the professional development of education researchers. In reality, these objectives are closely related. For example, we have treated issues related to the quality of research as largely applying to individual investigations of educational phenomena and issues related to the building of the knowledge base as applying to the long-term development of lines of inquiry over time. These concepts are intertwined and interdependent, however; the quality of individual studies cannot be understood separately from the broader lines of inquiry within which they are situated. The quality of education research can and should be viewed in the long term, and therefore, issues of how to frame and promote high-quality portfolios of work in key areas lead directly to questions of how to support the building of a coherent knowledge base from education research investigations over time. Furthermore, focusing on the professional development of education researchers during their doctoral work and throughout their careers requires that training and growth opportunities be provided in ways that reinforce high standards of quality and that promote an understanding of, and strategies for, integrating research across studies, subfields, disciplines, and theoretical paradigms (i.e., building the knowledge base).

To marshal both the intellectual and financial resources that will be required to implement these recommendations, individual members of the education research communities will need to support the ideas behind them in everyday interactions: in faculty meetings, in teaching, in writing funding proposals, in carrying out investigations, and, especially, in leadership positions. It is through this kind of grassroots dialogue and reinforcement about how to advance the field as a whole that the ethos and policies of the organizations we target will change to promote the committee's recommendations.

ISSUES FOR FUTURE CONSIDERATION

The committee's deliberations about ways to improve scientific research in education were necessarily limited by the topical areas featured in the committee's workshop series. In our view, these events raised important issues and suggested a set of strategic objectives to pursue that have great promise for advancing the field. These meetings were not designed, however, to cover all of the important issues facing the field today. We view our work as one in a series of steps that should be taken by members of the education research communities to reflect upon and advance their work and profession. In this section, we offer a few ideas of issues and problems to be taken up in such future efforts.

The report highlights the importance of the will of individual investigators to contribute to the kind of community building work we recommend be done: secondary analyses and replications; crossing disciplinary and institutional boundaries for doctoral training of researchers; engaging in consistent efforts to take stock of what is known; and dedicating substantial time to conducting and participating in peer review systems. We have suggested that the institutional incentive structures that shape the types of activities individual investigators choose to pursue at best tend to devalue these efforts, and at worst, they erect formidable barriers to engaging a cadre of talent in this crucial work. For example, few grant-making organizations support important yet costly syntheses or replications (preferring "new" investigations); major academic journals similarly discourage attempts to reanalyze data or otherwise extend previous work; investigators are hesitant to share their data because of the cost of preparation, the risk of someone else publishing from their data before they have the opportunity of doing so, and concerns about protecting the rights of research participants; and cross-disciplinary projects and endeavors require a considerable expenditure of energy that rarely "count" toward faculty tenure or promotion and that may not result in publication as lead authors in elite disciplinary journals critical to professional advancement. These are serious issues that require serious analysis and reconsideration of core principles and policies.

A second area worthy of investigation has to do with the relationship between the "supply" of education research and the "demand" for it by educators. This metaphor is featured frequently in discussing aspects of evidence-based education; indeed, we use it in the opening chapter to describe the parameters of our own work. In reality, however, the concepts of quality (supply) and utility (demand) are related and, in many cases, interdependent. Several workshop discussions illustrated this idea clearly: in discussing quality criteria and the types of expertise needed on peer review panels, for example, consideration of whether and how practitioners and stakeholders should be involved led immediately to a tangle of questions about how to think about quality in an applied field like education. Discussions about the role of partnerships between researchers and educators, and our recommendations regarding their encouragement and development, underscore the interdependence of both groups of professionals in promoting both high-quality research and research that has utility for schools. The successful implementation of research designs, and thus the validity of the conclusions drawn from the research, depends heavily on building relationships, establishing trust, and designing studies to advance both research purposes and the long-term needs of schools and school districts. Finally, the dual purpose of training future leaders in education and in education research within schools of education was characterized as a double-edged sword: the marriage can meaningfully embed the complex issues of practice into research conceptualization, implementation, and interpretation; but it can also slow the development of discipline-like norms and practices among researchers. We think in-depth consideration of such issues at the nexus of quality and utility in education research is needed.

The mix of researchers and educators in the training programs in schools of education not only highlights the important and complex ties between quality and utility, but it also raises issues about the training and participation of practitioners in education research. In our deliberations about the role of doctoral programs in schools of education, we made a strategic decision to focus on those schools that trained education researchers, recognizing that not all schools have such programs. However, improvements in education research also depend on the development of a profession in education practice that understands, values, and authenticates research. There are important questions about whether and how teacher and administrator candidates should be trained in the conduct or use of education research.

A final issue we deem worthy of in-depth consideration in future work pertains to the role and selection of journal editors in peer-reviewed education research publications. Our deliberations on this topic suggest that this key position be conceived as one that not only heavily influences the nature and quality of published work, but that also furthers the professional development of the field. From the handful of editors we heard from in the workshop series, the logistical burdens placed on education research journal editors seemed to far outstrip those of their peers at social and behavioral science journals. These burdens exact a hefty price: without adequate resources to support an efficient and effective editorial process, editors cannot devote their time to focus on the critical substantive responsibilities they have in promoting high-quality scholarship or to develop the professional capacities of the field. And easing the burden of editorship in education research journals would help to expand the talent pool of people who could be editors: for example, qualified investigators from small, typically cash-strapped universities, could more feasibly participate. Attending to these resource issues and carefully planning selection processes for editorships are critical issues worthy of further consideration.

CONCLUSION

The committee presents its recommendations while recognizing the hard work and investment of scarce resources that lies ahead to make progress toward advancing scientific research in education. We believe that it is a fundamental professional responsibility for individual investigators to contribute their talent and time to developing the core capacity of their community. It is in this spirit that we call on education researchers to focus on pursuing objectives that serve the common goals of the field: promoting research quality, facilitating the development of an accumulated knowledge base, and enhancing professional development.

This is a time of unprecedented opportunity for the various institutions and individuals who make up the field to initiate bold reforms. The enthusiasm—and angst—surrounding recent calls for "scientifically based research" can and should be harnessed to advance scientific research in education. The time to act is now.

References

Ad Hoc Working Group for Critical Appraisal of the Medical Literature. (1987). A proposal for more informative abstracts of clinical articles. *Annals of Internal Medicine, 106*(4), 598-604.

American Anthropological Association. (2004). *American Anthropological Association statement on ethnography and Institutional Review Boards.* [Adopted by AAA Executive Board June 4] . Arlington, VA: Author. Available: http://www.aaanet.org/stmts/irb.htm [Retrieved November 2004].

American Sociological Association. (1999). *Code of ethics and policies and procedures of the ASA Committee on Professional Ethics.* Washington, DC: Author.

Borman, W.C. (1979). Format and training effects on rating accuracy and rater errors. *Journal of Applied Psychology, 64,* 410-421.

Bradburn, N. (2003). *Remarks.* Presented to the National Research Council Committee on Research in Education Workshop on Understanding and Promoting Knowledge Accumulation in Education: Tools and Strategies for Education Research, June 30, Washington, DC. Transcript available: http://www7.nationalacademies.org/core/Remarks%20by%20Norman%20Bradburn.html.

Carnine, D. (2000). Why education experts resist effective practices (and what it would take to make education more like medicine). Available: http://www.edexcellence.net/doc/carnine.pdf/ [Retrieved July 29, 2004].

Chubin, D.E., and Hackett, E.J. (1990). *Peerless science: Peer review and U.S. science policy.* Albany: State University of New York Press.

Cicchetti, D.V. (1991). The reliability of peer review for manuscript and grant submissions: A cross-disciplinary investigation. *Behavioral and Brain Sciences, 14,* 119-186.

Cicchetti, D.V. (2003). *Remarks.* Presented to the National Research Council Committee on Research in Education Workshop on Peer Review of Education Research Grant Applications, February 26, Washington, DC. Transcript available: http://www7.nationalacademies.org/core/Cicchetti_ remarks.html.

81

Cicchetti, D.V., and Conn, H.A. (1976). A statistical analysis of reviewer agreement and bias in evaluating medical abstracts. *Yale Journal of Biological Medicine, 45*, 373-383.

Cohen, D. (2003). *Remarks*. Presented to the National Research Council Committee on Research in Education Workshop on a National Conversation About Doctoral Programs for Future Leaders in Education Research, November 12, Washington, DC. Transcript available: http://www7.nationalacademies.org/core/Cohen_Remarks_Research.html.

Cole, J.R., and Cole, S. (1981). *Peer review in the National Science Foundation: Phase two of a study*. Washington, DC: National Academy Press.

Coleman, J.S., Campbell, E.Q., Hobson, C.J., McPartland, J., Mood, A.M., Weinfeld, F.D., and York, R.L. (1966). *Equality of educational opportunity*. Washington, DC: U.S. Office of Education, National Center for Education Statistics.

Coughlin, B. (2003). *Remarks*. Presented to the National Research Council Committee on Research in Education Workshop on the Role of Journals in Developing the Education Research Knowledge Base, November 11, Washington, DC. Transcript available: http://www7.nationalacademies.org/core/journal_standards_workshop_agenda.html.

Cronbach, L.J. (with Shapiro, K.). (1982). *Designing evaluations of educational and social programs*. San Francisco: Jossey Bass.

Cronbach, L.J., Ambron, S.R., Dornbusch, S.M., Hess, R.D., Hornik, R.C., Phillips, D.C., Walker, D.F., and Weiner, S.S. (1980). *Toward reform of program evaluation*. San Francisco: Jossey Bass.

Daniel, H.D. (1993). *Guardians of science: Fairness and reliability of peer review* (translated by W.E. Russey). New York: VCH.

Ehrenberg, R., and Brewer, D. (1995). Did teachers' verbal ability and race matter in the 1960's? Coleman Revisited. *Economics of Education Review 14*(1), 1-21.

Ehrenberg, R., Goldhaber, D., and Brewer, D. (1995). Do teachers' race, gender and ethnicity matter? Evidence from NELS88. *Industrial and Labor Relations Review, 48*(3), 547-561.

Eisenhart, M. (2002). The paradox of peer review: Admitting too much or allowing too little. *Research in Science Education, 32*(2), 241-255.

Eisenhart, M., and Towne, L. (2003). Contestation and change in national policy on "scientifically based" education research. *Education Researcher, 32*(7), 31-38.

Emihovich, C. (2003). *Remarks*. Presented to the National Research Council Committee on Research in Education Workshop on the Role of Journals in Developing the Education Research Knowledge Base, November 11, Washington, DC. Transcript available: http://www7.nationalacademies.org/core/journal_standards_workshop_agenda.html.

Erickson, F., and Gutierrez, K. (2002). Culture, rigor, and science in educational research. *Educational Researcher, 31*(8), 21-24.

Golde, C., and Walker, G. (2002). *Overview of the Carnegie initiative on the doctorate*. Available: www.carnegiefoundation.org/CID/CID_Overview.pdf [Retrieved July 29, 2004].

Grissmer, D. (2003). *Remarks*. Presented to the National Research Council Committee on Research in Education Workshop on Understanding and Promoting Knowledge Accumulation in Education: Tools and Strategies for Education Research, June 30, Washington, DC. Transcript available: http://www7.nationalacademies.org/core/Remarks%20by%20David%20Grissmer.html.

Gueron, J. (2003). *Remarks*. Presented to the National Research Council Committee on Research in Education Workshop on Randomized Field Trials in Education: Implementation and Implications, September 24, Washington, DC: Transcript available: http://www7.nationalacademies.org/core/Gueron_Remarks.html.

Hackett, E.J., and Chubin, D.E. (2003). *Peer review for the 21st century: Applications for educational research.* Paper prepared for the Workshop on Peer Review of Education Research Grant Applications, National Research Council, February 25-26, Washington, DC. Available: http://www7.nationalacademies.org/core/Peer%20Review.html.

Hancock, C. (2003). *Remarks.* Presented to the National Research Council Committee on Research in Education Workshop on a National Conversation About Doctoral Programs for Future Leaders in Education Research, November 12, Washington, DC. Transcript available: http://www7.nationalacademies.org/core/Hancock_Remarks_Research.html.

Harding, S. (1991). *Whose science? Whose knowledge? Thinking from women's lives.* Ithaca, NY: Cornell University Press.

Harnad, S. (1998). The invisible hand of peer review. *Nature* (November 5).

Hartley, J. (1997). Improving the clarity of journal abstracts in psychology: The case for structure. *Science Communication, 24*(3), 366-379.

Hauenstein, N.M.A. (1998). Training raters to increase the accuracy and usefulness of appraisals. In J. Smither (Ed.), *Performance appraisal: State of the art in practice* (pp. 404-444). San Francisco: Jossey Bass.

Howe, K. (2004). A critique of experimentalism. *Qualitative Inquiry, 10*(1), 42-61.

Institute of Medicine. (2001). *Crossing the quality chasm: A new health system for the 21st century.* Committee on the Quality of Healthcare in America. Washington, DC: National Academy Press.

Iyengar, S., and Greenhouse, J.B. (1988). Selection models and the file-drawer problem. *Statistical Science, 3*, 109-135.

Kaestle, C.F. (1993) The awful reputation of education research. *Educational Researcher, 22*(1), 26-31.

Kellam, S.G. (2000). Community and institutional partnerships for school violence prevention. In *Preventing school violence* (vol. 2, NCJ 180972, pp. 1-21). Plenary Papers of the 1999 Conference on Criminal Justice Research and Evaluation-Enhancing Policy and Practice Through Research. Washington, DC: National Institute of Justice.

Kemper, K.J., McCarthy P.L., and Cicchetti D.V. (1996). Improving participation and interrater agreement in scoring Ambulatory Pediatric Association abstracts. How well have we succeeded? *Archives of Pediatric and Adolescent Medicine, 150*(4), 380-383.

Knorr-Cetina, K. (1999). *Epistemic cultures: How the sciences make knowledge.* Cambridge: Harvard University Press.

Labaree, D. (2003). *Remarks.* Presented to the National Research Council Committee on Research in Education Workshop on a National Conversation About Doctoral Programs for Future Leaders in Education Research, November 12, Washington, DC. Transcript available: http://www7.nationalacademies.org/core/Labaree_Remarks_Research.html.

Lagemann, E.C. (2000). *An elusive science: The troubling history of education research.* Chicago: University of Chicago Press.

Levin, J.R., and O'Donnell, A.M. (1999). What to do about educational research's credibility gaps? *Issues in Education, 5*(2), 177-229.

Levine, F. (2003). *Remarks.* Presented to the National Research Council Committee on Research in Education Workshop on a National Conversation About Doctoral Programs for

Future Leaders in Education Research, November 12, Washington, DC. Transcript available: http://www7.nationalacademies.org/core/Levine_Remarks_Research.html.

McKeown, M. (2003). *Remarks.* Presented to the National Research Council Committee on Research in Education Workshop on the Role of Journals in Developing the Education Research Knowledge Base, November 11, Washington, DC. Transcript available: http://www7.nationalacademies.org/core/journal_standards_workshop_agenda.html.

Mosteller, F., Nave, B., and Miech, E.J. (2004). Why we need a structured abstract in education research. *Educational Researcher, 3*(1), 29-34.

Myers, D. (2003). *Remarks.* Presented to the National Research Council Committee on Research in Education Workshop on Randomized Field Trials in Education: Implementation and Implications, September 24, Washington, DC. Transcript available: http://www7.nationalacademies. org/core/Myers_Durno_Remarks.html.

National Research Council. (1985). *Sharing research data.* Committee on National Statistics. Commission on Behavioral and Social Sciences and Education. Washington, DC: National Academy Press.

National Research Council. (1999). *Improving student learning: A strategic plan for education research and its utilization.* Committee on a Feasibility Study for a Strategic Education Research Program. Commission on Behavioral and Social Sciences and Education. Washington, DC: National Academy Press.

National Research Council. (2000). *Protecting data privacy in health services research.* Committee on the Role of Institutional Review Boards in Health Services Research Data Privacy Protection, Division of Health Care Services. Washington, DC: National Academy Press.

National Research Council. (2002). *Scientific research in education.* Committee on Scientific Principles for Education Research. R.J. Shavelson and L. Towne (Eds.). Center for Education, Division of Behavioral and Social Sciences and Education. Washington, DC: National Academy Press.

National Research Council. (2003a). *Sharing publication-related data and materials: Responsibilities of authorship in the life sciences.* Committee on the Responsibilities of Authorship in the Biological Sciences. Board on Life Sciences, Division on Earth and Life Studies. Washington, DC: The National Academies Press.

National Research Council. (2003b). *Strategic education research partnership.* Committee on a Strategic Education Research Partnership. M.S. Donovan, A.K. Wigdor, and C.E. Snow (Eds.). Division of Behavioral and Social Sciences and Education. Washington, DC: The National Academies Press.

National Research Council. (2004a). *Implementing randomized field trials in education: Report of a workshop.* Committee on Research in Education. L. Towne and M. Hilton (Eds.). Center for Education, Division of Behavioral and Social Sciences and Education. Washington, DC: The National Academies Press.

National Research Council. (2004b). *Strengthening peer review in federal agencies that support education research.* Committee on Research in Education. L. Towne, J.M. Fletcher, and L. Wise (Eds.). Center for Education, Division of Behavioral and Social Sciences and Education. Washington, DC: The National Academies Press.

Natriello, G. (2003). *Remarks.* Presented to the National Research Council Committee on Research in Education Workshop on Understanding and Promoting Knowledge Accumulation in Education: Tools and Strategies for Education Research, June 30, Washington, DC. Transcript available: http://www7.nationalacademies.org/core/Remarks%20by%20Gary%20Natriello.html.

Pulakos, E.D. (1986). The development of training programs to increase accuracy on different rating forms. *Organizational Behavior and Human Decision Processes, 38*, 76-91.

Raudenbush, S. (2003). *Remarks.* Presented to the National Research Council Committee on Research in Education Workshop on a National Conversation About Doctoral Programs for Future Leaders in Education Research, November 12, Washington, DC. Transcript available: http://www7.nationalacademies.org/core/Raudenbush_Remarks_Research.html.

Redish, E. (2003). *Remarks.* Presented to the National Research Council Committee on Research in Education Workshop on Peer Review of Education Research Grant Applications, February 25, Washington, DC. Transcript available: http://www7.nationalacademies.org/core/Redish_remarks.html.

Rothsein, H. (2003). *Remarks.* Presented to the National Research Council Committee on Research in Education Workshop on the Role of Journals in Developing the Education Research Knowledge Base, November 11, Washington, DC. Transcript available: http://www7.nationalacademies.org/core/Rothstein_Remarks_Journal.html.

Sackett, D.L., Richardson, W.S., Rosenberg, W., and Haynes, R.B. (Eds.). (1997). *Evidence-based medicine: How to practice and teach EBM.* London: Churchill Livingstone.

Schneider, B. (2003). *Remarks.* Presented to the National Research Council Committee on Research in Education Workshop on Understanding and Promoting Knowledge Accumulation in Education: Tools and Strategies for Education Research, June 30, Washington, DC. Transcript available: http://www7.nationalacademies.org/core/Remarks%20by%20Barbara%20Schneider.html.

Seastrom, M. (2003). *Remarks.* Presented to the National Research Council Committee on Research in Education Workshop on Understanding and Promoting Knowledge Accumulation in Education: Tools and Strategies for Education Research, June 30, Washington, DC. Transcript available: http://www7.nationalacademies.org/core/Remarks%20by%20Marilyn%20Seastrom.html.

Sebba, J. (2003). *Remarks.* Presented to the National Research Council Committee on Research in Education Workshop on the Role of Journals in Developing the Education Research Knowledge Base, November 11, Washington, DC. Transcript available: http://www7.nationalacademies.org/core/Sebba_Remarks_Journal.html.

Shadish, W.R., Cook, T.D., and Campbell, D.T. (2002). *Experimental and quasi-experimental designs for generalized causal inference.* Boston: Houghton-Mifflin.

Shulman, L. (2003). *Remarks.* Presented to the National Research Council Committee on Research in Education Workshop on a National Conversation About Doctoral Programs for Future Leaders in Education Research, November 12, Washington, DC. Transcript available: http://www7.nationalacademies.org/core/Shulman_Remarks_Research.html.

St. Pierre, E.A. (2002). "Science" rejects postmodernism. *Educational Research, 31*(8), 25-27.

Tobin, J. (2003). *Remarks.* Presented to the National Research Council Committee on Research in Education Workshop on a National Conversation About Doctoral Programs for Future Leaders in Education Research, November 12, Washington, DC. Transcript available: http://www7.nationalacademies.org/core/Tobin_Remarks_Research.html.

Towne, L. (in press). Scientific evidence and inference in educational policy and practice: Defining and implementing "scientifically based research." In C. Dwyer (Ed.), *Measurement and research in the accountability era*. Orinda, CA: Lawrence Erlbaum Associates.

U.S. Department of Education. (2002). *Strategic plan 2002-2007*. Washington, DC: Author. Available: http://www.ed.gov/about/reports/strat/plan2002-07/plan.pdf/ [Retrieved November 24, 2003].

U.S. Department of Education. (2004). *Improving teacher quality state grants, Title II, Part A: Non-regulatory guidance*. Available: http://www.ed.gov/programs/teacherqual/guidance.pdf/ [Retrieved July 13, 2004].

VandenBos, G. (2003). *Remarks*. Presented to the National Research Council Committee on Research in Education Workshop on the Role of Journals in Developing the Education Research Knowledge Base, November 11, Washington, DC. Transcript available: http://www7.nationalacademies.org/core/journal_standards_workshop_agenda.html.

Vaughn, S., and Damann, J.D. (2001). Science and sanity in special education. *Behavioral Disorders, 27*, 21-29.

What Works Clearinghouse. (2004). *Study design classification*. Available: http://www.w-w-c.org/about/workpapers.html/ [Retrieved July 19, 2004].

Whitehurst, G. (2003). *Remarks*. Presented to the National Research Council Committee on Research in Education Workshop on a National Conversation About Doctoral Programs for Future Leaders in Education Research, November 12, Washington, DC. Transcript available: http://www7.nationalacademies.org/core/Whitehurst_Remarks_Research.html.

Willinsky, J. (2003). *Remarks*. Presented to the National Research Council Committee on Research in Education Workshop on the Role of Journals in Developing the Education Research Knowledge Base, November 11, Washington, DC. Transcript available: http://www7.nationalacademies.org/core/Willinsky_Remarks_Journal.html.

Woehr, D.J., and Huffcutt, A.I. (1994). Rater training for performance appraisal: A quantitative review. *Journal of Occupational and Organizational Psychology, 67*, 189-205.

Zedeck, S., and Cascio, W.F. (1982). Performance appraisal decisions as a function of rater training and purpose of the appraisal. *Journal of Applied Psychology, 67*, 752-758.

Appendix A

Workshop Agendas

WORKSHOP AGENDA

Peer Review of Education Research Grant Applications:
Implications, Considerations, and Future Directions
February 25-26, 2003

Tuesday, February 25

8:30 a.m.
Welcome and Goals for Workshop
Lauress Wise, Chair, Committee on Research in Education and
President, HumRRO
Lisa Towne, Study Director, Committee on Research in Education

9:00 a.m.
Historical Context for Grants Peer Review
Edward Hackett, Arizona State University

10:15 a.m.
**Education Research and Peer Review: A Perspective from the Institute
of Education Sciences**
Grover (Russ) Whitehurst, Institute of Education Sciences, U.S.
Department of Education

11:00 a.m.

Goals and Purposes of Grants Peer Review: Perspectives from Investigators

   Hilda Borko, University of Colorado
   Penelope Peterson, Northwestern University
   Kenneth Dodge, Duke University
   Milton Hakel, Bowling Green State University
   Edward Redish, University of Maryland

1:45 p.m.

Peer Review Models: Perspectives from Funding Agencies

   Finbarr (Barry) Sloane, National Science Foundation
   Steven Breckler, National Science Foundation
   Brent Stanfield, U.S. Department of Health and Human Services
   Susan Chipman, Office of Naval Research
   Louis Danielson, U.S. Department of Education

4:30 p.m.

Selecting and Training Peers

   Teresa Levitin, U.S. Department of Health and Human Services
   Brent Stanfield, U.S. Department of Health and Human Services

Wednesday, February 26

8:30 a.m.

Report on Strengthening the Standards: An Evaluation of OERI Grants Peer Review

   Diane August, Center for Applied Linguistics
   Penelope Peterson, Northwestern University

10:15 a.m.

The Reliability of Peer Review for Grant Submissions

   Dominic Cicchetti, Yale University

11:15 a.m.

 Wrap-Up Discussion

WORKSHOP AGENDA

Workshop on Understanding and Promoting
Knowledge Accumulation in Education:
Tools and Strategies for Education Research
June 30-July 1, 2003

Monday, June 30

8:30 a.m.
Welcome and Goals for Workshop
> Lauress Wise, Chair, Committee on Research in Education and
> President, HumRRO
> Lisa Towne, Study Director, Committee on Research in Education

Part I. Knowledge Accumulation: What Does It Mean?

8:45 a.m.
Framing the Issues
> Kenji Hakuta, Stanford University
> Kenneth Howe, University of Colorado

> Moderated Discussion
> Jay Labov, National Research Council
> David McQueen, Centers for Disease Control and Prevention
> Sidney Winter, University of Pennsylvania

10:45 a.m.
Two Case Studies

**The Role of Resources in School and Student Performance
(a.k.a.: "Does Money Matter?")**
> Helen (Sunny) Ladd, Duke University
> David Cohen, University of Michigan

Culture and Learning
> Barbara Rogoff, University of California, Santa Cruz

Part II. Knowledge Accumulation: Tools and Strategies

1:15 p.m.

Common Core of Measures

    Barbara Schneider, University of Chicago

    Claudia Buchmann, Duke University

    Michael Nettles, University of Michigan

3:15 p.m.

Making Data Publicly Accessible

    Ronald Ehrenberg, Cornell University

    David Grissmer, RAND

    Gary Natriello, Teachers College

    Norman Bradburn, National Science Foundation

    Marilyn Seastrom, National Center for Education Statistics

Tuesday, July 1

8:30 a.m.

Ways of Taking Stock: Replication, Scaling Up, Meta-Analysis, Professional Consensus Building

    Hugh (Bud) Mehan, University of California, San Diego

    Robert Slavin, Johns Hopkins University

    Harris Cooper, University of Missouri-Columbia

    Lauress Wise, HumRRO

    Daniel Berch, National Institute of Child Health and Human

        Development

10:45 a.m.

Wrap-Up: Summary of Themes and Concluding Comments

    Lauress Wise, HumRRO

    Robert Floden, Michigan State University

WORKSHOP AGENDA

Randomized Field Trials (RFTs) in Education:
Implementation and Implications
September 24, 2003

8:30 a.m.
Workshop Objectives and Overview
> Lauress Wise, Chair, Committee on Research in Education and
> President, HumRRO
> Lisa Towne, Study Director, Committee on Research in Education

Session 1. RFTs in Context

8:45 a.m.
Nature of Education Research and Methodology
> Richard Shavelson, Stanford University

9:15 a.m.
Implementing RFTs in Social Settings
> Judith Gueron, MDRC

9:45 a.m.
Q&A

Session 2. RFTs in Educational Settings: Lessons Learned

10:45 a.m.
Case 1: Success for All After-School Program Study
> Olatokunbo (Toks) Fashola, Johns Hopkins University
> Loretta McClairn, Baltimore City Schools

11:15 a.m.
Case 2: Haan Foundation Study
> David Myers, Mathematica Policy Research
> Donna Durno, Allegheny Intermediate Unit

11:45 p.m.
Case 3: Baltimore Whole-Day First Grade Program Study
  Sheppard Kellam, American Institutes for Research
  Linda Chinnia, Baltimore City Schools

Session 3. Implications for Research and Practice

1:45 p.m.
Implications for Education Research and Researchers
  Robert Boruch, University of Pennsylvania
  Anthony (Eamonn) Kelly, George Mason University

2:15 p.m.
Q&A

3:15 p.m.
Implications for States
  Wesley Bruce, Indiana Department of Education

3:30 p.m.
Implications for Urban Districts
  Sharon Lewis, Council of the Great City Schools

3:45 p.m.
Implications for Traditionally Underserved Populations
  Vinetta Jones, Howard University

4:00 p.m.
Q&A

4:30 p.m.
Wrap-Up Discussion of Themes and Implications
  Kay Dickersin, Brown University

WORKSHOP AGENDA

The Role of Journals
in Developing the Education Research Knowledge Base
November 11, 2003

8:30 a.m.
Welcome and Overview
> Lauress Wise, Chair, Committee on Research in Education and
> President, HumRRO
> Lisa Towne, Study Director, Committee on Research in Education

Session 1. Defining the Territory

8:45 a.m.
> Barbara Schneider, University of Chicago and member of CORE

9:15 a.m.
Q&A

Session 2. Quality and Coherence in Publishing: A Roundtable

> Robert Floden, Michigan State University, Committee Moderator
> Bridget Coughlin, Managing Editor, *Proceedings of the National
> Academy of Sciences*
> Catherine Emihovich, (past) Editor, *Anthropology and Education
> Quarterly*
> Glenn Firebaugh, (past) Editor, *American Sociological Review*
> Lynn Liben, Editor, *Child Development*
> Margaret McKeown, Editor, *American Educational Research Journal*
> Gary VandenBos, Publisher, American Psychological Association

10:00 a.m.
Moderated Discussion: Focus on Quality

11:00 a.m.
Moderated Discussion: Focus on Coherence

Noon
Q&A

Session 3. Strategic Directions: Emerging Issues and Trends

Systematic Reviews
> Kay Dickersin, Brown University, Committee Moderator
> Judy Sebba, Department for Education and Skills, England
> Hannah Rothstein, Baruch College, City University of New York

1:30 p.m.
Presentations

2:15 p.m.
Q&A

Technology, Communication, and Audience
> Joseph Tobin, Arizona State University, Committee Moderator
> Gary Natriello, Columbia University
> John Willinsky, University of British Columbia

3:00 p.m.
Presentations

3:45 p.m.
Q&A

4:15 p.m.
Wrap-Up

WORKSHOP AGENDA

A National Conversation About Doctoral Programs for
Future Leaders in Education Research
November 12, 2003

8:30 a.m.
Welcome and Overview
> Lauress Wise, Chair, Committee on Research in Education and
> President, HumRRO
> Lisa Towne, Study Director, Committee on Research in Education

Session 1. Defining the Territory

8:45 a.m.
Institutional Context
> David Labaree, Stanford University

9:15 a.m.
Comparative Perspective
> Felice Levine, American Educational Research Association

9:45 a.m.
Q&A

Session 2. Analyzing Key Issues

10:45 a.m.
Developing a Common Curriculum
> Margaret Eisenhart, University of Colorado and member CORE

11:15 a.m.
Crafting Methodological Training
> Steven Raudenbush, University of Michigan

11:30 a.m.
Serving an Increasingly Diverse Talent Pool
> Charles Hancock, Ohio State University

11:45 a.m.

Relating Training to the Disciplines and Disciplinary Departments
Joseph Tobin, Arizona State University and member CORE

12:00 p.m.

Q&A

Session 3. Setting Strategic Directions

1:30 p.m.
Lee Shulman, Carnegie Foundation

2:00 p.m.
Grover (Russ) Whitehurst, U.S. Department of Education

2:30 p.m.
David Cohen, University of Michigan

3:15 p.m.

Moderated Discussion
Ellen Condliffe Lagemann, Harvard University and member of
CORE

4:15 p.m.

Q&A

Appendix B

Understanding and Promoting Knowledge Accumulation: Summary of Workshop Key Points

This appendix is a summary of Understanding and Promoting Knowledge Accumulation in Education: Tools and Strategies for Education Research, the second workshop in the series conducted by the Committee on Research in Education. The workshop featured a discussion of conceptual ideas about reflections, definitions, and challenges associated with knowledge accumulation, generalizability, and replication in education research. It also included a discussion of tools to promote an accumulated knowledge base derived from education research, many of which we highlight in our recommendations.

Rather than issue a separate report summarizing the workshop, the committee decided to develop a summary of key points that provide context for, and help illuminate, the conclusions and recommendations in this report. This decision was based on the recognition that the ideas discussed at this workshop—while by no means an exhaustive review of the philosophy of science or nature of education research—provide an important intellectual foundation for all of the issues and strategies that were discussed during the workshop as well as throughout the workshop series (see Appendix A for a compilation of agendas).

The workshop had two objectives. The first was to provide a context for understanding the concept of knowledge accumulation, both generally and with respect to education research. No one study or evaluation—no matter how rigorous—can single-handedly chart the path of progress for education policy and practice, nor can one study adequately sum up the state of understanding in a field or subfield. The challenge for research fields—including education research—is to find ways of facilitating the growth and refinement of knowledge about education phenomena over time. The second objective was to focus on concrete ways this progress of scientific knowledge in education research could be facilitated.

Thus, the workshop had two main parts: the first part featured a series of presentations and discussions designed to clarify phrases and terms like knowledge accumulation, generalizability, and replication in education. The second part featured discussions of three sets of tools for developing a more coherent body of knowledge from education research: developing common measures, sharing data, and taking stock of what is known. The appendix follows this structure, summarizing key points from each workshop part. Because much of what was discussed in the second part of the workshop— specific tools and strategies for promoting knowledge accumulation—is featured in boxes or in the conclusions and recommendations in the main body of the report, that section is significantly shorter than the first.

KNOWLEDGE ACCUMULATION: WHAT DOES IT MEAN?

Kenji Hakuta, in transition at the time of the event between Stanford University and the University of California, Merced, began the day with a presentation that considered key terms and ideas associated with knowledge accumulation and then traced the example of research in bilingual education to illustrate them. Following this overview, Kenneth Howe, of the University of Colorado focused on the interaction between the progression of scientific understanding and the methodological frameworks that researchers have utilized to study education. Reflecting on these two presentations, representatives from three disciplines and fields outside of education offered their perspectives on how the nature of knowledge accumulation in their fields is similar to and different from that in education: Jay Labov, of the National Research Council (NRC), on the biological sciences; David McQueen, of the Centers for Disease Control and Prevention, on epidemiology; and Sidney Winter, of the University of Pennsylvania, on business. Finally, two presentations that traced lines of inquiry in education research illustrated these core ideas with concrete examples: David Cohen, of the University of Michigan; and Helen (Sunny) Ladd, of Duke University, on the role of resources in school and student achievement; and Barbara Rogoff, of the University of California at Santa Cruz

Foundation Professor of Psychology, on the relationship between culture and learning.

Overall, the discussion made clear that knowledge accumulation, generalizability, and replication are terms that seem to have a straightforward meaning on the surface but are less clear when examined more closely. In general, presenters seemed to agree that knowledge accumulation is a way to think about the progress of scientific research—how investigators make sense of, and build on, the studies that shed light on particular phenomena. As Cohen clarified, however, it is more than just the "heaping up" of findings. It involves extending previous findings, including the elaboration and revision of accepted theories, with an eye always toward the growth of systematic understanding. In some cases, knowledge accumulation can involve wholesale replacement of a paradigm, as pointed out by McQueen.

The progression of scientific knowledge is described in *Scientific Research in Education* in these terms: "the path to scientific understanding . . . is choppy, pushing the boundaries of what is known by moving forward in fits and starts as methods, theories, and empirical findings evolve" (National Research Council, 2002). This first workshop session elaborated this core idea of methods, theories, and empirical findings interacting and growing in nonlinear ways.

Empirical and Theoretical Work

Several presenters described the dynamic relationship between theoretical or conceptual ideas in a field and the empirical studies that test their adequacy in modeling phenomena. Scientific understanding progresses when the field attends to both theoretical development and empirical testing and analysis; one without the other is not sufficient. Theory without empirical backing lacks real-world testing of its explanatory power. And data without theory leads to "dust-bowl" empiricism—that is, data that lack meaning or relevance to describing or modeling the phenomena of interest (teaching, learning, and schooling in education).

Rogoff provided the clearest illustration of how related lines of inquiry developed in cross-cultural psychology and sociolinguistics by researchers moving back and forth between periods of empirical investigation and theory building as one informed the other over time.

As she described it, in the 1960s and 1970s, there was a great deal of empirical investigation—about 100 studies—in the area of cross-cultural psychology (see Munroe, Munroe, and Whiting, 1981). This work applied cognitive tests in international settings and led researchers to question previous assumptions about the generalizability of developmental and learning theories that were dominant at the time. Through the multitude of studies conducted in this arena, it became clear that context mattered for evaluating learning.

Following that era, in which a great deal of empirical work was carried out, a period of theory-building ensued. During the late 1970s to the early 1990s, the field of cultural psychology developed a theory that allowed researchers to take context into account, rather than assuming that what was being examined was a window on general functioning. An influential event in this regard was the translation of Lev Vygotsky's work into English in 1978. It demonstrated how one could use both context and individual aspects of development in the same view. In short, his theory argued that individual development is a function of social and cultural involvements. Related cultural research with underserved populations in the United States also demonstrated the importance of considering the familiarity of the context in interpreting performance on cognitive tests and other contexts. Tests themselves are being investigated as a context with which some children are unfamiliar.

In her presentation on the role of resources in school and student achievement, Ladd demonstrated how different lines of inquiry in one broad area can emanate from different theoretical orientations or questions. She described three types of questions that have been prominent in this area of research:

1. What is the impact of school resources on educational outcomes? (The "effects" question.)

Ladd identified this question as the one addressed in the so-called education production function literature. In that literature, educational outcomes (defined as student achievement, educational attainment, or subsequent wage earnings) are typically modeled as a function of school inputs and family background characteristics (see, for example, the meta analyses by Hanushek [1986, 1997]). Such models have become increasingly sophisticated over time as a result of richer data sets and enhanced methodology. Notably missing from these models are teacher practices and institutional context. Hence, to the extent that particular practices are correlated with a specific school input, such as class size, across observations within a sample, the estimated impact of class size on student achievement reflects not only class size but also any teacher practices correlated with variations in class size.

2. What resources would be needed to achieve a particular desired educational outcome? (The "adequacy" question.)

Since the early 1990s, several economists have focused on this line of work, mainly using expenditure data at the district level. Emerging from this approach is the conclusion that some students, for example, those from low-income families, are more challenging to educate, and hence, require more resources to achieve a given educational outcome, than do students from more affluent families. (See, e.g., Duncombe and Yinger, in press; Yinger, 2004; Reschovsky, 1994; Reschovsky and Imazeki, 2003.) Research being conducted by Cohen, Raudenbush, and Ball (2002) also falls into this category of adequacy research. They start out with the notion of instructional goals, and then ask what instructional strategies are most productive in reaching those goals, how much these strategies cost, and, hence, what resources would be required.

3. What can be done to make a given level of resources more productive toward the goal of educational outcomes? (The "productivity" question.)

This line of research examines what can be done to make a given level of resources more productive in achieving educational outcome goals. Much of the effective schools literature of the 1970s and 1980s falls under this category (see Stedman, 1985, for a summary). In this line of work, researchers studied schools identified as being effective in raising achievement for disadvantaged students to determine what practices were common across effective schools. Ladd also identified other important work that addresses the productivity question, including Monk's (1992) discussion about the importance of investigating classroom practices and work summarized in Chapter 5 of the NRC report *Making Money Matter* (1999).

Method Matters

In addition to empirical observation and theoretical notions, a third dimension of the progression of research knowledge is the methods used to collect, analyze, and relate the data to the conceptual framework. Indeed, the main thesis put forth at the workshop by Howe was that questions concerning knowledge accumulation are difficult to disentangle from questions concerning broader methodological frameworks. He specifically argued that the experimental paradigm (that is, relying on random assignment designs) may encourage the accumulation of knowledge about easy-to-manipulate, simplistic instructional approaches. He also suggested that since experimental studies in education typically employ random assignment, rather than random selection (and thus are typically limited to those who volunteer), the generalizability of the findings is limited. Finally, he argued that experiments do not provide knowledge about the precise mechanisms of causal phenomena, which is necessary for deeper knowledge-building.

The exchange that followed the presentations extended the discussion of methodology by focusing on the need to use multiple methodologies in appropriate ways to promote broad understanding of the complexities of teaching, learning, and schooling over time. Using research on class size reduction as an example, Harris Cooper, who at the time of the workshop was in transition between the University of Missouri, Columbia, and Duke University, pointed out that examining the findings from small, qualitative studies opened up the "black box" and revealed that not only were teachers spending less time on classroom management and more time on instruction in smaller classes, but also that they were conducting more enrichment activities. This finding alerted the research community to a host of potential new effects that traditional quantitative research and the main findings about the effects of class size reduction on achievement would not—could not—have illuminated.

Later in the day, other speakers picked up the same theme. Hugh (Bud) Mehan, of the University of California, San Diego, provided an example of how the skillful combination of quantitative and qualitative methodologies is not only powerful but may also be necessary in education research. In describing his work in scaling up school improvement efforts beginning in a few schools in San Diego, extending to the state of California, and then growing yet again to multiple states, Mehan argued that the methodological approaches required to conduct the research on this program and its growth were both quantitative and qualitative. He suggested that although in individual investigations, quantitative and qualitative research are typically carried out independently, in carrying out large-scale studies in which programs are introduced and studied in increasing numbers of sites, this separation can no longer be sustained.

Public Interest and Contestation

Education research is often criticized for being endlessly contested, both among researchers and in the broader public community. Several participants mentioned the role of the public in shaping research, in both education and other fields, underscoring the point that public criticism is not unique to education and that this interest has both positive and negative effects.

Cohen argued most directly that education research both benefits and suffers as a field from high public interest. This level of involvement from the public can be trying for researchers as they try to balance their approaches to research on education issues with public concern that can often take on a highly political character. Public interest also lends the potential for greater success for the research field. The National Institutes of Health (NIH) have benefited greatly from the public demand for high-quality medical research in terms of rising appropriations. However, the high level of public interest in education is less productive for increasing the use of research findings, because the public places low value on research in education. While the public is highly interested in questions of how best to educate children, they rarely look to research to provide answers of value.

And there are opportunity costs associated with letting policy and political issues drive a research agenda. Hakuta's depiction of the bilingual education research following publicly framed dichotomies of program options—rather than research-driven, theoretically derived models based on practice—shows that this orientation led to a great deal of work trying to explain only a small fraction of the variation in how English-language learners best learn the language. Only recently, he argued, have researchers turned their attention to studies that focus on questions most relevant to understanding this key issue.

McQueen offered another example from research on the relationship between smoking and lung cancer. Ethical considerations obviously preclude randomly assigning people to smoke, so research findings were criticized as not being valid. Couple this fact with the involvement of interested parties (cigarette manufacturers, the antismoking lobby), McQueen posited, and research findings became even more contested. Winter offered another example from the realm of business, commenting that corporate governance is a "violently" contested area right now, with implications for research.

Finally, Labov elaborated that there are both internal and external controversies that play into claims regarding the contested nature of research. For example, in biology, evolution is an area that is hotly debated. Within the field, most biologists accept the idea of evolution as a key organizing principle of the discipline, but there is debate surrounding the mechanisms by which evolution occurs—such as Charles Darwin's idea of incremental change and Steven Jay Gould's idea of punctuated equilibrium. Outside the field, this debate is interpreted as a more serious controversy, and some outsiders suggest this as evidence that the theory of evolution itself is in question or is challenged by most biologists.

Contrasting Fields and Disciplines

An important contrast emerged with respect to the nature of theoretical ideas in fields of practice (like education and business) versus those in traditional scientific disciplines (like cell biology). McQueen articulated most explicitly that, in such applied fields as medicine and public health, theoretical ideas are different from those found in such disciplines as chemistry and biology. Medicine and public health are fields of action, he argued; as such, they are characterized by carrying out interventions, so practitioners draw on theories from multiple disciplines. He pointed out that when one works in a field rather than a discipline, it is difficult to set up a theoretical base whereby hypotheses and causal relationships are tested, as demanded by a more strict scientific model.

In his presentation, Hakuta provided a synopsis of the history of research on teaching students with limited English proficiency (LEP) that illustrated how education as a (contested) field of action influenced the creation of theoretical frameworks that shaped the associated field of research. In 1974, the Supreme Court decided in *Lau vs. Nichols* that addressing the needs of children who arrive in school not speaking English is a district and state responsibility. No particular approach was prescribed in the decision, so two general approaches for educating LEP students each developed a following: English-language immersion and a bilingual approach. LEP education became (and continues to be) a controversial issue; subsequently, a great deal of resources was invested in research to investigate the question of which was the better method. To date, the research shows a slight advantage in English-reading comprehension for LEP students who have been in transitional bilingual programs (see, e.g., Willig, 1985; Greene, 1998: National Research Council, 1997). However, comparatively very little research has focused on the gap in reading scores between LEP and non-LEP students and its growth as students progress through school. Specifically, in grade one, the gap in age equivalent scores of reading achievement between LEP and non-LEP students is equivalent to approximately one year in age. By fifth grade, that gap has increased to two years. Nothing in the research to date can explain that gap. Public pressure in the applied field of education, Hakuta argued, has led to an overemphasis on a single research question, inhibiting the growth of knowledge on other important questions.

In his discussion of research on the effects of resources on school and student achievement, Cohen pointed to another area in which a great deal of time and effort has been devoted to researching a phenomenon in the applied field of education research that accounts for a small percentage of the differences in student achievement. In describing research that explores the relationships among resources, instruction, and learning outcomes, Cohen began by summarizing the seminal *On Equality of Educational Opportunity*, known as the Coleman report, of 1966. Coleman investigated differences in performance among schools and concluded that resources made little or no difference. Since that report was released, there has been a great deal of additional investigation into this topic.

However, as Cohen pointed out, 80 percent of the differences in student achievement lie within schools, not from school to school, so there is a great deal of variation that is not being examined in this line of research. While research is ongoing in examining differences in both the 80 percent and the 20 percent, the public debate framed the question and the theoretical conceptions early, persisting for decades.

Context Dependence

Workshop speakers also argued that in a field like education, which is characterized by complex human interactions and organizational, cultural, and political influences, attending to context in the research process is critical. Thus, it is unreasonable to expect simple generalizations that are broadly applicable. That said, however, the field advances when investigators strive to make generalizations that build in descriptions of how context affects results. Furthermore, variation deriving from contextual factors is helping to reveal relationships: without variation, there is no way to learn about effects and patterns among variables and concepts. This context dependence is a theme that continued throughout the day, but in this session it became clear that it is not a characteristic that is unique to research in education.

In business, as Winter described, many situations depend on the interactions between employees, investors, and customers. These interactions can be quite complex and vary from one grouping to the next. As such, those who conduct research on business practices encounter many of the same obstacles in trying to understand the extent to which findings are applicable to multiple settings that education researchers do. In other words, the strategy that business researchers found was employed with resounding success in Site A may not be at all effective in Site B.

The importance of context dependence in the conduct of research is further demonstrated by the history of physiological experimentation at NIH. As Labov pointed out, NIH came under a great deal of criticism about 25 years ago because clinical trials were being conducted primarily on white male subjects. However, such results often do not generalize from one gender to the other. As a consequence, many of the treatments for diseases that affect both men and women, such as heart disease, were not as effective for women as they were for men, but without explicitly designing research to estimate differential effects on men and women, physicians would not know to prescribe different regimens.

In one sense, participants characterized the fact that results vary across contexts as a challenge to efforts that aim to make summary statements applicable to multiple settings, times, and populations. Mehan, for example, quipped that the one core principle of ethnographic work is "it depends," referring to this relationship between findings and contexts. However, explaining variation is the core purpose of research, so the variation that results from this context dependence also enables attempts to model differences in outcomes. Rogoff, echoed by a few other workshop participants, argued that the field of education ought to focus its efforts on elaborating theories and crafting "universal laws that account for this context dependence and thus reflect the complexity of educational phenomena."

Relationship to Practice

Extending the discussion of education and business as fields rather than disciplines, two dimensions of the relationship between practice and research were elaborated. First, David Klahr, of Carnegie Mellon University, when questioning the presenters, offered the idea that education research might be more comparable to an engineering discipline than a science. He continued by arguing that knowledge accumulates in engineering through practice. For example, there is a great deal of variability from one space shuttle to another, even though they are all in the same series. As one shuttle would be completed, he continued, engineers would apply what was learned in the construction of that shuttle to the design and construction of the next.

Second, a conversation about the role of cases in education and business research further elaborated the close link between practice and research in these fields. Cohen's description of a particular line of work in which he has been involved in the resources and student achievement area illustrated this idea in education. Along with his colleagues Steve Raudenbush and Deborah Ball, Cohen has spent considerable time examining the relationship between resources and student achievement. They have found that much of the research on school effects assumes a model in which there are desired outcomes that are directly caused by the input of resources. However, he argued, this is not plausible, because resources become active only when they are used. Therefore, in order to validly measure the effects of resources, the conditions in which they are used must be taken into account, and this requires attention to practice.

Winter also offered examples of how practice relates to research in business. First, he said that for students engaged in dissertation work, they are fortunate if they can carry out two or three years of work in an area without a merger or a regulatory incident interfering with their research site. He went on to say that the use of cases in business schools is to create effective managers that "more or less give people a vision of what it means to be pushing the levers that are available for controlling a management situation."

Continuing to explore the idea of how theoretical ideas and research priorities can and should be driven by the practices of the field (education, business, medicine, etc.) and their surrounding political contexts, Lauress Wise pointed out that most NRC studies that integrate and summarize research on a topic across disciplines and fields do so at the request of public officials and are therefore at least partially shaped by the political and policy questions of the day.

Two talks on scaling up brought into sharp relief how research and practice can feed into one another in ways that benefit both. Robert Slavin, of Johns Hopkins University and chairman of the Success for All Foundation, illustrated the potential for mutually reinforcing relationships between educational practice and research and evaluation by detailing the history of the development of the Success for All program. According to Slavin, by the 1970s a body of evidence about the effectiveness of cooperative learning pointed to the value of such student team approaches (see Slavin, 1995).

At the same time, the idea was gaining a foothold among practitioners, and so their use became commonplace. However, the fundamental elements that research suggested needed to be in place for them to promote learning—groups were structured, purposes were clear and shared by all students, and each member had a specific task or role to play—were typically not in place in practice. Slavin told the group that the research findings and the disconnect between them and what was going on in schools was the "intellectual background" for the development of Success for All, which began in one school in Baltimore and is now operating in about 1,500 schools across the country. As the program grew, Slavin and his team have engaged in a development process of implementing programs, studying how they are used and what their influences are, and then feeding that knowledge back into program improvement but also, importantly, into the larger knowledge base on cooperative learning, comprehensive school reform, and program evaluation.

Mehan, too, touched on this idea by offering a lesson from his experience in scaling up school reform efforts in California and the fact that the research that documented and analyzed the expansion was an iterative process. The iterations were necessary, he argued, to strike the right balance between a standard set of questions and data collection protocols and the need to recognize and articulate what he termed "emergent phenomena." Because program elements interact with local circumstances in different ways, Mehan argued that the kinds of issues and data that are relevant to understanding the implementation and effectiveness of the program will vary to some degree across sites.

Research Community

A final theme raised in this initial workshop session was the crucial role of the community of investigators, including funding agencies, to support efforts to integrate and build on findings from related work. Hakuta said it plainly: "It is not just the methods that enable knowledge to accumulate," but also fundamental are "the critiques and the questioning that happen in science."

While such critique and debate in a field is healthy and promotes the growth of knowledge, workshop speakers suggested that it is important to keep the debate at a civil level. One audience member noted that a tone of derisiveness and lack of respect can creep into the discourse, especially across disciplines, which is to the detriment of the kind of building community that can facilitate knowledge accumulation. Winter reiterated this point, suggesting that the kind of standards that would be most useful to researchers are standards for "intelligent debate."

One issue that is closely related to community is the lack of common quality standards in education research. Hakuta suggested that standards could be helpful, but he cautioned that standards generated within the community are much more likely to be accepted by researchers than standards that are imposed from the top down. Across workshop speakers, opinions on the topic varied, with some suggesting that standards would serve as an impediment to research, and others suggesting that standards would improve research quality. Rogoff cautioned that standardization could be premature; it could short-circuit the empirical work that needs to be carried out in order to learn more about the regularities across communities and across contexts that would enable the understanding of how culture plays a role in human development. To do this, she argued, lines of research that build on prior studies are needed, because from each study, questions, theories, and ways of doing research are refined.

Other speakers addressed the idea of human capacity in research and its connections to knowledge accumulation. Mehan, for example, discussed the need for thoroughly trained research staff—preferably those who have been working with the team on the issues for some time—to collect data according to protocols and to be attuned to what he called relevant "emergent phenomena" in scaling up and studying the implementation and effects of the Achievement Via Individual Determination, or AVID, program. In a different vein, Harris Cooper, in describing the evolution of meta-analytic methods for summarizing research on effectiveness about a particular intervention, argued that "vote counting"—a way of summarizing literatures commonly used by researchers—is a demonstrably poor method for arriving at valid conclusions about what the research says collectively (in that it consistently leads to an underestimation of the program effect), suggesting that researchers with meta-analytic skills are needed for these tasks.

The discussion of human capacity extended beyond individual investigators. Daniel Berch, of the National Institute of Child Health and Human Development, offered a description of the important role of federal research agency personnel in both taking stock of what is known in an area and in using that information for setting research priorities. Depicting the unique bird's eye view of the field or fields that agency staff has, Berch described a variety of activities that directors engage in as they work directly with leading investigators. These include such activities as assembling panelists to participate in workshops that consider the current state of knowledge and potential areas for breakthrough, and listening in on peer review panels on which scholars review proposals for new work—all of which coalesce to inform the ongoing development of research programs.

KNOWLEDGE ACCUMULATION: HOW TO PROMOTE IT

Barbara Schneider, of the University of Chicago, began the second part of the workshop by focusing on the idea of replication, a concept, she argued, that provides an important, unifying idea for creating scientific norms that can unite a community of researchers from different disciplinary perspectives. She asserted that replication begins with data sharing—it is the sharing of information about studies, including the actual data on which findings are based, that makes replication possible. Replication involves applying the same conditions to multiple cases, as well as replicating the designs, including cases that are sufficiently different to justify the generalization of results in theories, she said. Without convergence of results from multiple studies, the objectivity, neutrality, and generalizability of research are questionable.

In addition to addressing more specific topics, David Grissmer, of the RAND Corporation, provided important insights about strategies for knowledge accumulation in education research that explicitly relate theory, data, and measures and connect to the themes described in the previous section. He argued that generating consensus is not a matter of gathering more data or generating better techniques. "It is much more a matter of whether we can get replicable and consistent measurements across social science in general, and education, as a basis for forming theories." Until there are consistent measurements, he went on to say, it is not possible to build broader theories. Furthermore, it is the role of theory to cut down on the amount of data collected. "Without theory, you collect everything. With theory, you can design a very specific set of experiments to test." He argued that currently the field of education research is oriented toward making more measurements. As a result, "we have much research, but little knowledge." Grissmer suggested that progress depends on the field focusing much more on exploring and explaining why research results differ to enable nuanced generalizations that account for variations in findings and contexts.

Several of the ideas and strategies for promoting an accumulated knowledge base in education research discussed during the session are described in the main body of this report. A very brief synopsis of issues covered and speakers featured in each session is provided here.

Common Measures

Central to the conduct of research is the gathering of data on various measures. Common measures for the types of data collected by researchers can help to promote the accumulation of knowledge by facilitating the comparison and analysis of results across studies in both similar and disparate environments. In a session dedicated to this topic, two speakers elaborated on moving toward more common definitions of important measures in education research. Claudia Buchmann, of Duke University, discussed the development of measures of family background, including socioeconomic status. Michael Nettles, who at the time of the workshop was in transition between the University of Michigan and the Educational Testing Service, discussed issues surrounding the measurement of student achievement.

In her presentation, Buchmann offered a rationale for why measures of socioeconomic status and family background are important in education research and charted the progression of measure development that reflects the challenges of developing a common core of measures in education. She argued that family background measures are required to conduct a fair assessment of educational outcomes by enabling the isolation of outcomes from differences in inputs: student populations in different schools differ from the beginning, so it is necessary to control for this variation. Giving careful thought to how to measure family background relates to the necessity to improve knowledge of the ways that the family, as an institution, affects children's ability and motivations to learn and their academic achievement. The bulk of Buchmann's presentation focused on tracing the evolution of the concept of family background, which she demonstrated has become increasingly complex over time. She described simple socioeconomic status measures expanding to include an array of measures targeting different dimensions of this concept: for example, family structure or demographic characteristics, as well as family social and cultural capital. Buchmann also showed, compared, and critiqued how a sampling of major surveys and data collection efforts measured these concepts and their effects on the quality of inferences that could be drawn about key questions across and within them.

Nettles approached the idea of a common set of measures from a slightly different standpoint, focusing on the benefits and drawbacks of using the National Assessment of Educational Progress (NAEP) as a centralized measure of achievement. He argued that there is a great deal of fragmentation and questionable stability in measuring student achievement. Although NAEP is appealing for a number of reasons, Nettles raised a number of issues related to student motivation, representativeness across geographic areas and other categories, the validity of the test for making particular inferences, and equity and bias, that have significant bearing on research that relies on these measures of student achievement.

Data Sharing

Another set of tools or strategies that can facilitate the continued development of a coherent knowledge base is the sharing of data. In her introductory talk, Schneider pointed to three points of leverage for encouraging data sharing and replication: professional associations, scholarly journals, and data banks.

A panel that focused on data sharing followed consisted of five scholars from a range of positions and roles in the research community: individual investigators, senior officials from federal agencies, and journal editors. Ronald Ehrenberg, of Cornell University, discussed his experience using and reanalyzing the Coleman data. Grissmer focused on the role of NAEP. Marilyn Seastrom, of the National Center for Education Statistics, described the agency's efforts to maximize access to data while maintaining privacy and confidentiality. Norman Bradburn, of the National Science Foundation, extended Seastrom's presentation by focusing on broad concepts and tools associated with access, privacy, and confidentiality. And finally, Gary Natriello, of Teachers College, offered ideas on the role of journals in facilitating and promoting data sharing. Key points from these presentations are discussed in Chapter 3.

Taking Stock

The workshop concluded with a session focused on ways of taking stock—that is, efforts by researchers to summarize what is known in topic areas or subfields. In various ways, investigators in a field periodically assess what (they believe) they know and formally or informally integrate findings from individual studies into the larger body of knowledge. The practice of researchers attempting to replicate previous studies is one way to assess the extent to which findings hold up in different times, places, and circumstances. Similarly, a researcher who has piloted and evaluated a program at a small number of sites might scale up to a larger number of sites to see if and how results transfer to other settings. Research synthesis and meta-analysis are yet another way to summarize findings across studies of program effectiveness. Explicit efforts to engage groups of investigators (and other stakeholders) in building professional consensus can also generate summative statements that provide an indication of what is known and not known at a particular point in time.

Five speakers offered ideas for how the field can promote the accumulation of research-based knowledge through such work. Mehan and Slavin focused their talks on how scaling up programs or reform models to increasing numbers of schools offers opportunities for contributing to the advancement of scientific understanding while improving program services for participating schools. Cooper described meta-analysis, a methodology used to summarize the findings from multiple studies of program effects. Drawing on personal experience working with committees charged with developing consensus about research findings in areas of education, Wise described the consensus-building process of the NRC. Finally, Berch described the ways in which the National Institute of Child Health and Human Development attempts to understand what is known, what is not known, and how to craft research agendas and competitions based on that understanding.

The presenters seemed to agree that the accumulation of knowledge in education is possible, but challenging. The studies, methods, and activities they described together showed that careful, rigorous attempts to provide summative statements about what is known as a foundation for the continued advancement of scientific research in education are possible. To be sure, impediments exist. Cooper mentioned the tendency of advocacy groups to selectively rely on research results to support their (previously established) political positions and a lack of civility among researchers as particularly acute problems to be overcome. Summing up these sentiments, Cooper put it this way: "knowledge accumulation is possible, but it is not for the faint of heart."

REFERENCES

Cohen, D.K., Raudenbush, S.W., and Ball, D.L. (2002). Resources, instruction, and research. In F. Mosteller and R. Boruch (Eds.), *Evidence matters: Randomized trials in education research*, (pp. 80-119). Washington, DC: Brookings Institution Press.

Duncombe, W.D., and Yinger, J. (In press). How much more does a disadvantaged student cost? *Economics of Education Review.*

Greene, J.P. (1998). *A meta-analysis of the effectiveness of bilingual education.* Claremont, CA: Tomas Rivera Policy Institute.

Hanushek, E.A. (1986). The economics of schooling: Production and efficiency in public schools. *Journal of Economic Literature, 24,* 1141-1177.

Hanushek, E.A. (1997). Assessing the effects of school resources on student performance: An update. *Educational Evaluation and Policy Analysis, 19,* 141-164.

Monk, D.H. (1992). Education productivity research: An update and assessment of its role in education finance reform. *Educational Evaluation and Policy Analysis, 14*(4), 307-332.

Munroe, R.H., Munroe, R.L., and Whiting, B.B. (Eds.). (1981). *Handbook of cross-cultural human development.* New York: Garland STPM Press.

National Research Council. (1997). *Improving schooling for language-minority children: A research agenda.* Committee on Developing a Research Agenda on the Education of Limited-English-Proficient and Bilingual Students. D. August and K. Hakuta (Eds.). Washington, DC: National Academy Press.

National Research Council. (1999). *Making money matter: Financing America's schools.* Committee on Education Finance. H.F. Ladd and J.S. Hansen (Eds.). Commission on Behavioral and Social Sciences and Education. Washington, DC: National Academy Press.

National Research Council. (2002). *Scientific research in education.* Committee on Scientific Principles for Education Research. R.J. Shavelson and L. Towne (Eds.). Center for Education. Division of Behavioral and Social Sciences and Education. Washington, DC: National Academy Press.

Reschovsky, A. (1994). Fiscal equalization and school finance. *National Tax Journal, 47*(1), 185-197. [Reprinted in Joel Slemrod (Ed.). (1999). *Tax Policy in the Real World* (pp. 209-221). New York: Cambridge University Press.]

Reschovsky, A., and Imazeki, J. (2003). Let no child be left behind: Determining the cost of improving student performance. *Public Finance Review, 31*(3), 263-290.

Slavin, R.E. (1995). *Cooperative learning: Theory, research, and practice.* Boston: Allyn & Bacon.

Stedman, L.C. (1985). A new look at the effective schools literature. *Urban Education. 20*(3), 295-326.

Vygotsky, L. (1978). *Mind and society: The development of higher psychological processes* (M. Cole, V. John-Steiner, S. Scribner, and E. Souberman, Trans.). Cambridge, MA: Harvard University Press. (Original work published 1930.)

Willig, A.C. (1985). A meta-analysis of selected studies on the effectiveness of bilingual education. *Review of Educational Research, 55*(3), 269-317.

Yinger, J. (Ed.). (2004). *Helping children left behind: State aid and the pursuit of educational equity.* Cambridge, MA: MIT Press.

Appendix C

Biographical Sketches of Committee Members and Staff

Lauress L. Wise (*Chair*) is president of the Human Resources Research Organization (HumRRO). His research interests focus on issues related to testing and test use policy. He has served on the National Academy of Education's Panel for the Evaluation of the National Assessment of Educational Progress (NAEP) Trial State Assessment, as co-principal investigator on the National Research Council's (NRC) study to evaluate voluntary national tests, and as a member of the Committee on the Evaluation of National Assessment of Educational Progress (NAEP). He has been active on the NRC's Board on Testing and Assessment, the Committee on Reporting Results for Accommodated Test Takers: Policy and Technical Considerations, and the Committee on the Evaluation of the Voluntary National Tests, Year 2. At HumRRO, he is currently directing an evaluation of California's high school graduation test and a project to provide quality assurance for NAEP. Prior to joining HumRRO, he directed research and development on the Armed Services Vocational Aptitude Battery (ASVAB) for the U.S. Department of Defense. He has a Ph.D. in mathematical psychology from the University of California, Berkeley.

Linda Chinnia is an educator with the Baltimore City public school system. During a 32-year career, she has served as an early childhood teacher, a senior teacher, a curriculum specialist, an assistant principal, a principal, and the director of elementary school improvement. Currently she serves as an area academic officer, supervising 35 elementary and K-8 schools. She

115

has been an adjunct instructor at the Baltimore City Community College, Coppin State College, Towson University, and Johns Hopkins University. She has taught courses in early childhood education, elementary education, and educational supervision and leadership. She has B.A. and M.A. degrees from Towson University.

Kay Dickersin is a professor at the Brown University School of Medicine. She is also director of the U.S. Cochrane Center, one of 14 centers worldwide participating in The Cochrane Collaboration, which aims to help people make well-informed decisions about health by preparing, maintaining, and promoting the accessibility of systematic reviews of available evidence on the benefits and risks of health care. Her areas of interest include publication bias, women's health, and the development and utilization of methods for the evaluation of medical care and its effectiveness. She was a member of the Institute of Medicine's Committee on Reimbursement of Routine Patient Care Costs for Medicare Patients Enrolled in Clinical Trials, the Committee on Defense Women's Health Research, and the Committee to Review the Department of Defense's Breast Cancer Research Program. She has an M.S. in zoology, specializing in cell biology, from the University of California, Berkeley, and a Ph.D. in epidemiology from Johns Hopkins University's School of Hygiene and Public Health.

Margaret Eisenhart is professor of educational anthropology and research methodology and director of graduate studies in the School of Education, University of Colorado, Boulder. Previously she was a member of the College of Education at Virginia Tech. Her research and publications have focused on two topics: what young people learn about race, gender, and academic content in and around schools; and applications of ethnographic research methods in educational research. She is coauthor of three books as well as numerous articles and chapters. She was a member of the NRC's Committee on Scientific Principles in Education Research. She has a Ph.D. in anthropology from the University of North Carolina at Chapel Hill.

Karen Falkenberg is a lecturer in the Division of Educational Studies at Emory University. She is also the president of the Education Division of Concept Catalysts, a consulting company that has a specialization in science, mathematics, and engineering education reform. She works both nationally and internationally. She was the program manager for the National Science Foundation funded local systemic change initiative in Atlanta called the Elementary Science Education Partners Program (ESEP), and has been a mentor for *SERC@SERVE's* Technical Assistance Academy for Mathematics and Science and for the WestEd National Academy for Science and Mathematics Education Leadership. She also served on the National Academy of Engineering's Committee for Technological Literacy. Earlier, she was a high school teacher of science, mathematics, and engineering and was featured as a classroom teacher in case studies of prominent U.S. innovations in science, math, and technology education. Before she became an educator, she worked as a research engineer. She has a Ph.D. from Emory University.

Jack McFarlin Fletcher is a professor in the Department of Pediatrics at the University of Texas-Houston Health Science Center and associate director of the Center for Academic and Reading Skills. For the past 20 years, as a child neuropsychologist, he has conducted research on many aspects of the development of reading, language, and other cognitive skills in children. He has worked extensively on issues related to learning and attention problems, including definition and classification, neurobiological correlates, intervention, and most recently on the development of literacy skills in Spanish-speaking and bilingual children. He chaired the National Institute for Child Health and Human Development (NICHD) Mental Retardation/Developmental Disabilities study section and is a former member of the NICHD Maternal and Child Health study section. He recently served on the President's Commission on Excellence in Special Education and is a member of the NICHD National Advisory Council. He has a Ph.D. in clinical psychology from the University of Florida.

Robert E. Floden is a professor of teacher education, measurement and quantitative methods, and educational policy and is the director of the Institute for Research on Teaching and Learning at Michigan State University. He has written on a range of topics in philosophy, statistics, psychology, program evaluation, research on teaching, and research on teacher education. His current research examines the preparation of mathematics teachers and the development of leaders in mathematics and science education. He has a Ph.D. from Stanford University.

Ernest M. Henley is a professor emeritus of physics at the University of Washington. He has served as the dean of the College of Arts and Sciences at the University of Washington and as director and associate director of its

Institute for Nuclear Theory. The focus of his work has been with space-time symmetries, the connection of quark-gluons to nucleons-mesons, and the changes that occur to hadrons when placed in a nuclear medium; at present he is working in the area of cosmology. He was elected to membership in the NAS in 1979 and served as chair of its Physics Section from 1998-2001. He is a Fellow of the American Academy of Arts and Sciences, and served as president of the American Physical Society and as a member of the U.S Liaison Committee for the International Union of Pure and Applied Physics. He has a Ph.D. in Physics from the University of California, Berkeley.

Vinetta C. Jones is an educational psychologist and the dean of the School of Education at Howard University. During a 30-year career in public education, she has maintained a singular focus: developing and supporting professionals and creating institutional environments that develop the potential of all students to achieve high levels of academic excellence, especially those who have been traditionally underserved by the public education system. She has written and lectured widely on issues related to the education of diverse populations, especially in the areas of academic tracking, the power of teacher expectations, and the role of mathematics as a critical factor in opening pathways to success for minority and poor students. She served for eight years as executive director of EQUITY 2000 at the College Board, where she led one of the largest and most successful education reform programs in the country. She has served on numerous boards and national committees and was inducted into the Education Hall of Fame by the National Alliance of Black School Educators in 2000. She has a B.A. from the University of Michigan and a Ph.D. in educational psychology from the University of California, Berkeley.

Brian W. Junker is professor of statistics, Carnegie Mellon University. His research interests include the statistical foundations of latent variable models for measurement, as well as applications of latent variable modeling in the design and analysis of standardized tests, small-scale experiments in psychology and psychiatry, and large-scale educational surveys such as the NAEP. He is a fellow of the Institute of Mathematical Statistics, a member of the board of trustees and the editorial council of the Psychometric Society, and an associate editor and editor-elect of *Psychometrika*. He also served on the NRC's Committee on Embedding Common Test Items in State and District Assessments. He is currently a member of the Design and

Analysis Committee for NAEP. He has a Ph.D. in statistics from the University of Illinois (1988).

David Klahr is a professor and former head of the Department of Psychology at Carnegie Mellon University. His current research focuses on cognitive development, scientific reasoning, and cognitively based instructional interventions in early science education. His earlier work addressed cognitive processes in such diverse areas as voting behavior, college admissions, consumer choice, peer review and problem solving. He pioneered the application of information-processing analysis to questions of cognitive development and formulated the first computational models to account for children's thinking processes. He was a member of the NRC's Committee on the Foundations of Assessment. He has a Ph.D. in organizations and social behavior from Carnegie Mellon University.

Ellen Condliffe Lagemann is the Charles Warren Professor of the History of American Education and dean of the Harvard Graduate School of Education. Dr. Lagemann has been a professor of history and education at New York University, taught for 16 years at Teachers College at Columbia University, and served as the president of the Spencer Foundation and the National Academy of Education. She was a member of the NRC's Committee on Scientific Principles in Educational Research. She has an undergraduate degree from Smith College, an M.A. in social studies from Teachers College, and a Ph.D. in history and education from Columbia University.

Barbara Schneider is a professor of sociology at the University of Chicago. She is a codirector of the Alfred P. Sloan Center on Parents, Children and Work and the director of the Data Research and Development Center, a new federal interagency initiative designed to build research capacity. Her current interests include how social contexts, primarily schools and families, influence individuals' interests and actions. She has a Ph.D. from Northwestern University.

Lisa Towne (*Study Director*) is a senior program officer in the NRC's Center for Education and adjunct instructor of statistics at the Johns Hopkins University Institute of Policy Studies. She has also worked for the White House Office of Science and Technology Policy and the U.S. Department of Education Planning and Evaluation Service. She received an M.P.P. from Georgetown University.

Joseph Tobin is a professor in the College of Education at Arizona State University. Previously he served as a professor in the College of Education at the University of Hawaii. His research interests include educational ethnography, Japanese culture and education, visual anthropology, early childhood education, and children and the media. He was a member of the NRC's Board on International Comparative Studies in Education. He has a Ph.D. in human development from the University of Chicago.

Tina M. Winters (*Research Associate*) works in the NRC's Center for Education. Over the past 10 years, she has worked on a wide variety of education studies at the NRC and has provided research assistance for several reports, including *Scientific Research in Education, Knowing What Students Know*, and the *National Science Education Standards*.